D1530459

Behavioural Science in Industry

Behavioural Science in Industry

Richard I. Drake   Peter J. Smith

London · New York · St Louis · San Francisco · Düsseldorf · Johannesburg · Kuala Lumpur
Mexico · Montreal · New Delhi · Panama · Paris · São Paulo · Singapore · Sydney
Toronto

Published by
McGRAW-HILL Book Company (UK) Limited
MAIDENHEAD · BERKSHIRE · ENGLAND

07 084418 6

Printed and bound in Great Britain.

Contents

Preface

The problem the authors experienced in writing this book was one of too much information. Recently the amount of work which has been carried out in the area covered by the broad heading of Behavioural Science in Industry has increased very rapidly. In handling this information, therefore, there has inevitably been a degree of selection of material which reflects the biases and interests of the authors. Nevertheless, an attempt has been made to be as wide ranging as possible in sources of material.

The book is arranged in two parts. Experience of talking to people about the behavioural sciences has shown that a considerable communication problem exists. Indeed probably more than half the battle in understanding what behavioural science can do will be won if the reader has a 'feel' for what behavioural science is. Chapters 1 to 6, therefore, are concerned with exploring what behavioural science is. The chapters cover a wide range, from attempts at defining behavioural science (chapter 1), through a discussion about methods used (chapter 2), to a closer look at some of the basic concepts which behavioural scientists use (chapter 3).

Three key areas are then explored further as, in the opinion of the authors, they are crucial to an appreciation of the subject. The first key area explored is the relationship between man and work, which is broadly described throughout its history before devoting closer attention to the present view (chapter 4); the second is present thinking about group behaviour, which is considered in some detail (chapter 5); and the third, the systems approach to viewing organizations (chapter 6).

Chapter 7 functions as a 'half way house' where an attempt is made to examine ways in which problems in organizations can be appreciated, and in doing this the concepts explored in the earlier chapters are used.

The remaining chapters develop some specific areas of behavioural science and its use in industry. People are looked at in terms of how they lead and want to be led (chapter 8), and also with respect to the growing need to acquire new social skills if they are to be effective in organizations (chapter 9). Job and organizational design is explored (chapter 10) and finally a chapter is devoted to the highly misunderstood term, organizational development, (chapter 11).

The authors hope they have succeeded in preparing a book which managers will find of use, not so much as a series of prescriptions, but as a way of handling the complexity of organizational behaviour. It is not comprehensive but, it is hoped, it is comprehensible.

Our thanks are due to Tavistock Publications Ltd for permission to publish short extracts from *The Study of Society* by Alfred Kuhn (in chapter 2), *Behavioural Worlds* by P. G. Herbst (in chapter 4), *Form and Content in Industrial Democracy* by F. E. Emery and E. Thorsrud, and *Systems of Organization* by E. J. Miller and A. K. Rice; to Harvard University Press for permission to quote from *Management and the Worker* by F. J. Roethlisberger and W. J. Dickson (in chapter 5); and to the Longman Group Ltd for permission to quote from *Organizational Development* by P. J. Sadler and B. A. Barry (in chapters 5 and 11).

Finally, Patricia O'Brien, of the Tavistock Institute's secretarial staff, must be gratefully thanked for all the work she has willingly carried out in the preparation of this book.

Richard I. Drake
Peter J. Smith

What is behavioural science?

Behavioural science as a subject has developed because it has not been possible to retain the traditional distinctions between various disciplines such as psychology, sociology, and anthropology when attempting to solve practical problems in industry and other social institutions. Many different levels of explanation are valid for any one phenomenon and it has been necessary to apply theories and concepts which belong to other behavioural disciplines. Behavioural scientists, particularly those working in the industrial sphere, have demonstrated that solutions derived solely from the framework of one discipline have proved inadequate. Understanding of the performance of an organization cannot come from behavioural studies alone, but must refer to other disciplines, such as economics and operational research.

Within the behavioural sciences themselves, human behaviour can be explained at a number of different system levels—and to some extent these levels coincide with other disciplinary boundaries. These systems can be arranged as in Fig. 1.1.

SYSTEM LEVEL	ELEMENTS	EXAMPLE	DISCIPLINES
SOCIETY	A system of institutions and their relationships	UK	SOCIOLOGY and ANTHROPOLOGY
INSTITUTION	A system of organizations and their relationships	'Private Sector'	
ORGANIZATION	A system of groups and their relationships	Xy company	
GROUP	A system of roles and their relationships	A group of production managers	
ROLE	A system of expectations as to appropriate behaviour	A production manager in Xy company	SOCIAL PSYCHOLOGY
PERSONALITY	A system of attributes, experiences, abilities, and dispositions which give an individual his unique adaptation to the environment	A 'type' of person, e.g. extroverted, analytical, intelligent, dominant, etc.	PSYCHOLOGY
ORGANISM	A system of organs	Human body	

Fig. 1.1   *Different levels of viewing behaviour*

This is a simple account, but it helps to separate the various levels at which behaviour may be studied. In medicine, for example—the study of the human organism—it is possible to focus on molecules, cells, organs, and groupings of organs; and at each level it is also possible to focus on the interdependence of these parts. The behavioural scientist has borrowed from the biological sciences to provide himself with a similar model for ordering and analysing the relationships between component parts of society. Although this model of the functional interdependence of parts attracts criticism, it is a useful way of appreciating the many influences which determine human behaviour and the social context in which it takes place.

PSYCHOLOGY   The discipline of psychology is mainly concerned to explain and predict individual behaviour by reference to the nature of the individual. Psychology's main focus is upon individual differences (e.g., intelligence, attitudes) and processes (e.g., perception, motivation) which help to explain varying responses to similar situations or stimuli. Like all sciences it has developed methods to measure these differences and processes. Thus some psychologists study personality structure and the factors in personality which can usefully be used to differentiate people and predict their behaviours in a given situation. The level of intelligence, the degree of extroversion or introversion, dominance or submissiveness, calmness or excitability, and the propensity to neuroticism, among other factors, are used to describe individual personality differences. Psychologists seek general theories about attitude formation, perception, motivation, learning, growth and adjustment etc., which indicate the generality of attributes and processes in individuals; and they also study the conditions and causes of individual variability. In their study of these aspects of individual behaviour and individual differences, psychologists are more concerned than other behavioural scientists to examine the influence of inheritance, genetic mutation and segregation, congenital and constitutional influences. They thus have a close relationship to the physiological, biological and medical sciences.

In common with other behavioural sciences, psychology has many sub-disciplines and a major one is social psychology. Social psychologists extend the knowledge of individual differences and processes into a study of their significance in the social environment, and how the environment interacts with, and influences them. Other significant sub-disciplines include educational psychology, clinical psychology, and occupational psychology. While a great deal of psychology, as a total science, is relevant to the world of work, it is the occupational psychologist who is most often the practitioner psychologist in organizations. In this role he will be active in recruitment, selection (including ability and personality testing), counselling, appraisal, job design, attitude surveys, communication studies, and training activities.

Sociology as a discipline is much less 'person-centred'. It develops theories and makes predictions about social groupings and wider social processes. The description and explanation of social values, social change, deviant behaviour, religious behaviour, and patterns of family life, are typical examples. It directs its concern not at differences between individuals, but at differences which exist between 'collections' of individuals (social classes, political groups, occupational groupings). Although science aims at prediction, some sociological work is in the main descriptive, outlining patterns of social activities and differences both verbally and numerically. From such descriptive studies often come the hypotheses about social phenomena which enable sociologists to study and explain them further, e.g., the causal relationships between social class and educational opportunity, between organization structure and communication, between family pattern and urban environments, between technology and management structure. Although these examples may appear as simple one-to-one relationships, in reality the sociologist is often dealing with a range of complex interdependent social processes, all of which have to be considered in order to understand a particular social phenomenon. In this respect, sociology has been unable to take itself into the laboratory, where it can isolate the relative weight of causal influences by experimental method. This too inhibits the quantification desirable in all sciences and explains why sociological explanation is frequently hypothetical.

While many sociologists have been concerned with major social processes—institutions and organizations—some have worked in the field of small group behaviour. They have come nearest to conventional experimental method in their attempts to isolate the structural variables in groups (e.g., size, role structure) and their influences on group and member behaviour.

In the industrial sphere, sociologists who concern themselves with organization look at internal characteristics such as organization structure, wages systems, technology and work flow, formal and informal patterns of organization relationships, communications, industrial relations, management values and attitudes; and the character of external relationships between the organization, its members, and the wider environment. In the latter, sociologists examine such social factors as occupational and social mobility and changing population characteristics.

ANTHROPOLOGY Anthropology, one of the earliest of the behavioural sciences, traditionally was distinguished by the study of whole communities and societies, particularly those popularly referred to as 'primitive' societies, since non-industrial, relatively small and simple communities enabled the anthropologist to lay bare the broad functions of complete units. It was from the work of the early anthropologists that 'models' of social units were developed, most particularly that of functional interdependence, which enabled social scientists to understand the complex interrelatedness of social groupings and social processes. While much of contemporary anthropology still concentrates on simple societies, anthropologists also work at the level of an industry, the industrial firm, and its relationship to the community. Studies of whole industrial communities, in coal-mining[1] and fishing[2], for instance, have provided descriptions and analyses of the relationship between work and life.

AN INTER-DISCIPLINARY APPROACH Managers are concerned with the task of the organization and its achievement, so as to ensure the organization's survival and growth. The study of organizational behaviour requires that all levels of explanation of causes and interacting influences are borne in mind to appreciate more fully the nature of individual behaviour, and social process within (and acting on) the organization. Seeking to manipulate one level (for instance, individual motivation, group behaviour, organizational structure, or management style), without being aware of the interrelated sets of effects that such manipulation will have within the organization in terms of its ability to cope with market conditions and to negotiate transactions across its boundaries, is potentially dangerous. For instance, the psychologist's explanation that frustration at work is induced by low levels of decision-making is inadequate unless it is coupled with a sociological enquiry into the market conditions in which the organization must survive, and the technology it employs, which may place constraints upon its capacity to meet individual needs. Similarly, any application of sociological theories would be incomplete without studying the effects these changes might have upon individual motivation and attitudes.

4

This brief introduction to behavioural science should stress that:

(a) A 'total system' approach to organizational change and development is the right one. Loudly heralded panaceas which concern themselves only with particular aspects of a total system are at best partial solutions to the problems of organizations, and at worst cause much more trouble than they are worth.

(b) Many of the distinguishing characteristics of an organization are but a reflection of the constraints which its environment places upon it. The very fact that existing organization has 'survived' so far, at least indicates a partially relevant adaptation to its environment.

THE IMPORTANCE OF HUMAN RESOURCES

A manager must frequently observe, predict, expect, and ask for certain behaviour or activities from other people. Few managers have much formal knowledge of human behaviour, yet the accuracy of prediction, and extent of co-operation and co-ordination among people is remarkably high. Generally, attempts are made to understand behaviour by reference to personal reasons and beliefs. This may lead to misinterpretation and inaccurate prediction about the behaviour of others owing to personal biases and prejudices. Popularly held 'lay' theories of behaviour are generally incomplete and highly oversimplified, and very often 'common-sense' assumptions about human behaviour are wrong, or have not adjusted to changing circumstances.

People—human resources—constitute the most valuable resource of any organization, since without them the physical resources of buildings, materials and machines would be inoperable and, in the final analysis, irrelevant. It is significant that 'human asset worth' is not written into any balance sheet, yet a large amount of what is done represents an investment in people. When it is considered that the replacement cost of someone in an organization is very substantial, it is surprising that an accounting method has not been developed to incorporate this worth into a statement of a company's health[3]. While figures will vary according to industry and region and country, there is general agreement that labour turnover costs approximately £150 for a semi-skilled operative, and, at least, a year's salary for an executive. Attempts to measure the asset worth of an organization's human resources, put it between three and ten times the annual wage and salaries bill.

The managing of human resources is only now emerging as a critical management activity. In the past, man was often viewed as a dependent and inanimate resource to be manipulated according to production and market demands, and in many instances he was treated as a machine. Even today this is demonstrated by many assembly line and routine clerical operations. In a social and economic climate where human resources were plentiful, where skill was not at such a premium, where working hours were long, and international competition a fraction of what it is today, where the standard of education was low, representation weak, and communications slow, the management of human resources remained generally unskilled.

Slowly this mechanistic view of man has been forced to change. Increasing wealth and the increasing distribution of wealth (brought about by 'mechanistic man's' effort) have led to a rise in the cost of labour. At the same time technological advance has increased the capital intensity of industry. Therefore, progressively more highly paid people at all levels are in charge of more of an organization's (and ultimately society's) resources. In this situation the consequences of withdrawal of effort (either obviously by strikes, or less obviously by avoidance of decision making) are much more serious than they were in the days of mechanistic man. Today, therefore, people are concerned about alienation from work, not because alienation is a new phenomenon, but because the consequences of it, in economic, social, and human terms, are more serious than ever before.

Partly for this reason the increase of thought and investigation into people's motivation at work has been considerable. The broad conclusion reached, though not necessarily accepted, is that if people are treated as people at work, rather than as extensions of machines, then alienation and withdrawal will not be experienced. *Treating people as people* is a meaningless statement unless it is explored and explained further. A body of knowledge and experience has developed which implies that people can be motivated in their work both by the nature of the task itself and by aspects of their work environment. Values and expectations brought into the work place from the environment influences a person's orientation and hence his motivation to work.

There are two opposed trends in the work environment. First, peoples' level of knowledge, awareness, and understanding are growing with developments in education and communication; second, many jobs are being de-skilled through the removal of decision-making and other known 'satisfying' activities, because of technical and economic imperatives. This growing divergence gives rise to human and organizational problems, some of which the manager is called upon to anticipate and to resolve. While there should be concern about the consequences for the individual of a poor match between his abilities and those demanded by his job, the social and economic consequences of widespread under-employment are all too obvious. In any country with few natural resources, the major national resource is people, and it is essential that they are employed to their full potential. The changes implied by these conclusions affect the structure of, and processes within organizations and also the traditional pattern of authority in the organization—and indeed in society. No clear universally applicable alternative organizational forms exist, and never will, since the organization needed varies with the task, its technology and the culture and expectations of its employees. Thus, while broad conclusions point in a general direction of change, the variability of any situation requires a tempering of the universality of some findings with an empirical and practical approach.

The marshalling of knowledge within the disciplines comprising the behavioural sciences has allowed convincing predictions to be made about the nature of man and the environment he creates. The requirements for ensuring effective work performance in organiz-ations are changing rapidly and on a large scale, as people become better educated and less work orientated. The behavioural scientists must therefore consider what forms of organizations might be developed to employ effectively large groups of people who are not compelled to work for reasons of scarcity, and who are increasingly leisure orientated. An absorbing exploration of the changing values in western society is provided by Gurth Higgin in *Symptoms of Tomorrow*[4].

BEHAVIOURAL SCIENCE AND ORGANIZ-ATIONS

How is wealth to be created and distributed? Such considera-tions are the beginning of the study, development, and application of present forms of organization, in order to identify those which are the most appropriate for anticipated future conditions. The behavioural scientist finds himself involved in job and organiz-ational design from the point of view of, both, the psychological requirements of individuals at work and the sociological require-ments of organizations and institutions.

Behavioural science is vital in enabling organizations to deal more effectively with the present and with the future. It does this at two levels. First, it helps to interpret changes in the environ-ment in such a way as to allow the organization to appreciate what is happening and to do something about it. Second, behavioural science helps in the task of *changing* organizations to cope with environmental demands. It is concerned therefore both with

7

interpretation and action. Behavioural science is not the only science which is of help to organizations, but it is the one which is especially concerned with the human resources. The problems of man living and working with man are emerging as critical issues for the second half of the twentieth century.

REFERENCES

(1) Denis, N., Henriques, F., and Slaughter, C., *Coal is our life*, Eyre and Spottiswoode, 1956.
(2) Tunstall, J., *The fishermen*, MacGibbon and Kee, 1969.
(3) Saunders, D., 'How much is a manager worth? *Industrial Training International*, **6**, 2, 1971.
(4) Higgin, G. W., *Symptoms of tomorrow*. Plume Press—Ward Locke, London, 1973.

2
Methods and problems

A scientist and his friend were driving through Wyoming and saw a flock of sheep up on mesa.
'They've just been sheared,' said the friend.
'They seem to be, on this side,' replied the scientist.[1]

In the previous chapter the boundaries of the various disciplines normally referred to as the behavioural sciences were outlined, but the use of the word 'science' was not discussed. A science is based on a systematic body of knowledge which is cumulative and which enables it to explain or predict the relationships between a number of phenomena. Should the predictions prove correct in all cases that have been observed, knowledge of the relationship assumes the status of a law. A scientific law is a brief statement which tells of the relationship that has always been found to exist between a number of observed quantities of a defined kind. Thus the law of gravity states that, in all cases studied, the force of attraction between two bodies has been found to be directly proportional to the sum of their masses and inversely proportional to the square of the distance between them.

Science, however, does not consist solely of laws. It consists also of a large body of 'knowledge' which enjoys much less certainty and reliability in its power to predict events. Theories, and at a lower degree of reliability, hypotheses, make up the bulk of scientific knowledge. These statements of relationships between phenomena are normally at a much lower level of generality than the laws and hedged around by a multitude of qualifying factors.

Many sciences are considered such because they have general laws. The law of thermodynamics, Boyle's law, or in a social science, the law of diminishing returns, are examples. (The status of a law is such that any case of a phenomenon which seemed to disagree with it would initially be assumed to have been incorrectly observed.) The behavioural sciences do not have at this time an established body of laws which constitute irrefutable bases. Many people find this disappointing. They expect the behavioural sciences to give unambiguous general statements about the causation of behaviour. In so far as behaviour has an organic, or neuro-physiological explanation, this is so, but when attempts are made to explain behaviour in a socially meaningful way, one is confronted by complexity. The interdependence of many factors appear to be influencing the many aspects of behaviour itself. A measure of the extent of this complexity can be appreciated from the various 'system' levels of behaviour outlined in the previous chapter. Alfred Kuhn[2] has noted that although many of the factors involved in the causation of behaviour are understood and that many of these can be stated fairly precisely, when confronted with an example of behaviour to be interpreted, analysed, and explained, the very large numbers of factors involved produce uncertainty as to relative significance of any single factor.

> In the realm of psychology and the social sciences we now understand many of the forces which mould human behaviour. Many of these bits of understanding, taken one at a time, are quite as precise as many of the laws of chemistry and physics. The thing that seems to make the social sciences so 'unscientific' is that a large number of such forces are in action simultaneously in almost every individual event, and we have no way of knowing in advance which one, or even which few, will dominate. One of the commonest errors on this score is to assume that uncertainty of this sort is the peculiar property of the *social* scientists. It is not. To illustrate, suppose that we tell a physicist that at precisely noon on March 13, 1980 we will release a feather from a plane flying due east over the Statue of Liberty at ten thousand feet and 600 miles per hour. Not a scientist on earth would risk a dime, much less his reputation, predicting when and where (within a hundred yards) the feather would land. Nor could any physicist after the most thorough study tell you where any particular atom in a piece of steel will be one second after he completes his study, or how fast it will be travelling.

The behavioural sciences are still in the stage of developing their basic models of behaviour, and in doing so some of their observations, statements and explanations may sometimes seem obvious. In attempting to determine basic laws of behaviour, behavioural scientists are working in the area of individual life experience, and most people have an awareness of these basic laws, although this awareness is at an intuitive and inarticulated level. This is why behavioural scientists are often accused of 'blinding statements of the obvious'. But, frequently, scientists find themselves confronting established, accepted beliefs with scientifically derived information which shows the common-sense 'obvious' assumption to be in error, for example, the demonstration that the earth is round and Galileo's demonstration that objects of different weight fall at the same velocity. In the behavioural sciences such upsets to popularly held beliefs are less spectacular but not uncommon. In *The American Soldier*[3] for example, some assumptions which were made about American soldiers were found to be invalid. It was not true that the recruits from farms would tolerate hardship better than urban recruits, or that better educated soldiers showed more mental instability in combat. *The Affluent Worker in the Class Structure*[4] examined the assumption that as some worker incomes rise to a level equal and in excess of many middle class incomes, the affluent worker would acquire middle class social values—a process known as 'embourgeoisement'. The authors' found that 'middle-class social norms are not widely followed nor middle-class life-styles consciously emulated; and assimilation into middle-class society is neither a proven norm . . . a desired objective.'

It is important that science should be sceptical of common sense assumptions.

> You do not take anything for granted when you enter a monastery of science. You take the vow of scepticism until the evidence comes in. This is contrary to normal human thinking, which abhors explanatory vacuums[1].

Science requires rigour in the methods by which it acquires its knowledge. The words it uses should be clearly defined to make it possible for others to understand their meanings. Its methods of data collection should be impartial and the requirements of objectivity carefully observed in interpretations of the data and relationships between phenomena.

It is possible to have an *invalid* argument with a *true* conclusion, and a *valid* argument with an *untrue* conclusion. Scientists are only interested in valid arguments, those which are conducted according to the criteria of scientific method. While many decisions taken daily are based upon limited evidence and illogical arguments and contain much subjective feeling, the scientist, in his role of pursuing valid arguments and true conclusions, observes the principles of objectivity and logical reasoning. Scientific method is a means to the acquisition of information which can then be regarded as scientifically respectable and from which predictions can be made. It ensures a systematic, objective, and amongst scientists an agreed (or relatively so) manner of description, explanation, and prediction of phenomena.

11

The behavioural sciences do not differ greatly in their methods from those adopted by the physical and natural sciences, and their activities seek to pass through the same basic phases. These are,

the *observation* of phenomena
the *classification* of phenomena
the *prediction* of a relationship between phenomena
the *verification* through data collection and interpretation
and finally, a *generalization* which establishes the validity of the correlation or the causal relationship.

(A correlative relationship is: X is consistently associated with Y. A causal relationship is: X is caused by Y. It is very easy and dangerous to confuse correlative relationships with causal ones.)

METHODS IN BEHAVIOURAL SCIENCE

Most managers come into contact with the behavioural sciences when an organization has an apparently pertinent problem. The following are the basic steps which would typically be taken by a behavioural scientist in a problem-solving context.

Exploratory Investigation

This would include discussion with the management who are controlling the behavioural scientists' activities and with those who are concerned with the particular problem.

Attempts would be made to determine the boundaries of the problem and to compare the perceptions that individuals and group have of it. This process normally culminates in the next step which is—

Reformulation of the Problem

This spells out the problem in behavioural science terms and may bring into consideration new and unexpected factors for examination. Discussions would probably take place to secure agreement on the nature of the problem and to clarify the role of the behavioural scientist in any further investigation.

Development of Hypotheses

Agreement on the general problem will now require specific aspects of the problem to be isolated for investigation. Technically, an hypothesis is a cause and effect statement but in this form of scientific investigation the 'hypothesis' may simply isolate a phenomenon for investigation.

Plan Collection of Data

The statement of hypotheses is important to ensure the appropriate and economic collection of data. In part, however, what data are or could be available might determine the hypotheses. A special skill of the behavioural scientist is his ingenuity in developing means of acquiring relevant data.

The primary methods of data collection are:

(a) Interviews and discussions with relevant personnel, including group discussions.
(b) Questionnaires.
(c) The observation of relevant activities, either as an 'external' observer, or as a participant observer.
(d) The use of the records available in the organization.

This process involves the classification and interpretation of the information obtained and its comparison to the hypotheses. It may reveal the need for further data collection of a similar or different kind.

Findings are normally both a description and an explanation of the problem. They are usually incorporated into a written report, but may also be fed back verbally and through group discussions. It is likely that some recommendations for action (PRESCRIPTION) will be included.

These steps are logical and rational, but people tend not to be logical and rational. The behavioural scientist in an organization may be seen as a threat to people in that organization and 'behind the scenes' moves are sometimes made to prevent the behavioural scientist doing what he has been asked to do. For example, the manager of a department with a high labour turnover may feel threatened when a behavioural scientist arrives to look at the labour problems, and may try to withhold the relevant information.

The problem which a behavioural scientist is asked to help solve may be only an excuse for a 'hidden' management problem. The introduction of a behavioural scientist may, for example, be a way of neutralizing someone else's authority in the organization. Then too, management may believe that the introduction of a behavioural scientist has of itself solved the problem.

In such situations the behavioural scientist must be able to recognize such hidden problems so that he knows what steps he can take. He may withdraw or he may try to get the real problem more in the open. The processes involved in the *re-formulation of the problem*, therefore, will not necessarily be logical and rational, but could involve an exploration of emotional and irrational issues.

The use of behavioural science to diagnose and prescribe for existing problems, such as labour turnover, or poor work performance, ignores the scientist's potential role in the planning and design of management activity. These stages are vital in problem *prevention.* Many behavioural scientists are called in when conventional approaches, such as work study or training, have failed. In these circumstances the potential usefulness of behavioural science is severely reduced. There is the danger that behavioural scientists working in industry will concentrate on problem-solving and upon the development of quick remedies rather than furthering the body of scientific knowledge, which is of long-term importance to management as well as to society and the behavioural scientist.

Not all organizations use behavioural science in the immediate problem-solving role. Some organizations have employed behavioural scientists to work with them to explore wider issues such as 'what kind of organization do we need for the future'. Here, the behavioural scientist is given a wider brief in which the early stages of exploration and re-formulation are generally lengthy and involve the total organization and its environment.

SOME PROBLEMS PECULIAR TO BEHAVIOURAL SCIENCE
Experimental Method

Many sciences make progress in the amount of knowledge which is accumulated by designing experiments which can be closely controlled and repeated in conditions of isolation. Experimental method requires that the experimenter holds a number of factors unchanged while changing just one. From this he is able to observe the effect of the change of one factor on the others. In the behavioural sciences this method is usually difficult to apply because of the complexity and indivisibility of the subject matter. A good example is the evaluation of training. The problem of really knowing what the effect of training has been lies in defining the effects of factors such as market fluctuations, shifts in morale, plant maintenance problems, what competitors have been doing, changes in public opinion, and government legislation. Holding these other variables still (assuming one has isolated them) while changing the nature of the training in order to measure its effect, is patently impossible.

Observer Effect

Most sciences study the inanimate. The 'life' sciences concerned with lower forms of living matter do not face the problems of the understanding which the subject of the research may have about the purpose of the experiment. Those concerned with studying animal behaviour will have similar problems. 'Higher' animals are aware of the presence of the experimenter or observer and this influences the behaviour of the animal.

The discovery of the 'observer effect' with people (see chapter 4, 'The Hawthorne Studies') provided the behavioural scientist with an awareness of his problems. A behavioural scientist with a questionnaire is aware that however carefully he had designed his questions, the respondent's behaviour, perceptions, attitudes, etc., will be influenced by the very fact that he is being questioned, especially if the subject is important to him. Being asked for opinions about one's job, for instance, can produce a favourable response simply because someone is going to the trouble of finding out.

A further problem for the behavioural scientist is that he has to contend with his own values, attitudes, and perceptions, which will cause him to select, consciously or unconsciously, what he regards as relevant. In physical sciences this is an equal problem, for one can generally find facts to prove a theory. This is why science often insists that rather than collecting data to validate a hypothesis, the scientist should collect data to disprove it. In the behavioural sciences, the desire to prove a hypothesis may also be mixed up with feelings about the matter being studied. Empathy, sympathy, and identification are valuable human qualities—but they can seriously influence the selection of information, the analysis of it, and the manner in which it is used to 'test' hypotheses.

The influence of values on data collection is apparent in the interview, one of the most widely used information gathering techniques. A classic study by Stuart Rice[5] demonstrated the effect of an interviewer's values on the type and interpretation of information gathered. He had twelve people interview 2000 homeless men to find out the reason for their condition. Of these twelve interviewers, one was an ardent prohibitionist and another a strong socialist. The findings of these two interviewers are summarized in Fig. 2.1.

There is, however, no reason why values and feelings should not be involved in the solution of problems, provided there is a clear understanding of what these biases are and that at a critical phase

INTERVIEWER	Percentage of men reported by the interviewer as attributing their condition to	
	ALCOHOL	INDUSTRIAL SITUATION
PROHIBITIONIST	34	43
SOCIALIST	11	60

Fig. 2.1   *Findings from the interviewer bias study*

in the process of problem-solving, scientific objectivity is adhered to. The three broad phases to scientific problem-solving are:

(1) the selection of the problem to be solved and development of hypotheses,
(2) the collection, analysis, and interpretation of information,
(3) the recommendations for action.

The first and last stages will inevitably involve values, feeling, and judgements on the part of the scientist. It is the middle phase which requires vigilance regarding the way in which attitudes and values affect the collection and interpretation of data.

REFERENCES

(1) Chase, S., *The Proper Study of Mankind*, New York: Harper, 1948.
(2) Kuhn, A., *The Study of Society: a Multi-disciplinary Approach*, Tavistock Publications, 1966.
(3) Stouffer, S. A., and others, *The American Soldier.* (2 vols.) Princeton: Princeton University Press, 1949.
(4) Goldthorpe, J. H., and others, *The Affluent Worker in the Class Structure*, Cambridge University Press, 1969.
(5) Rice, S. A., 'Contagious Bias in the Interview', *American Journal of Sociology,* **35**, 1929.

3
Some concepts used in behavioural sciences

The language of the behavioural scientist is sometimes difficult to understand. What may appear to be a collection of jargon terms has developed and this can and does lead to considerable problems of communication. The meanings of some of the terms which are commonly used by behavioural scientists, terms which managers will inevitably encounter as they explore this field, are set out briefly below. The terms chosen, although by no means exhaustive, cover a range of concepts as applied to the individual, the group, and the organization.

Behaviour is a widely used word applied to individuals, animals, groups, organizations, etc. In this book the main concern is with the behaviour of the individual, who will normally be active in response to some stimulus. It is this general reaction that gives rise to the concept of behaviour. People 'behave' in varying and often characteristic ways. Often it can be said 'that's typical of Brown'. The determination of behaviour therefore can be found in the demands placed on the individual by his environment, and also by what sort of 'person' he is—the effects of his upbringing and his inherited characteristics. This raises the heredity/environment argument, and today it appears the pendulum is swinging away from the Victorian notion of 'man is born' to one where it is considered that the reason for much of our behaviour is to be found in the environment. The nature/nurture argument, however, may be irrelevant since both nature and nurture are highly interdependent elements of behaviour causation. None the less it is important to know, where possible, the relative weight of these influences if realistic plans for the change and development of organization and individuals are to be made.

BEHAVIOUR

The behaviour of an individual at any one time is the result of the demands placed upon him by his environment, and his internal 'state'. This state derives from the interplay between all his

THE INDIVIDUAL
(a) Personality

17

previous experience and his genetic inheritance. Over a period of time this state is regarded as an individual's 'personality'. Personality is the term most commonly used to label, in a global way, that collection of behaviours that go together to make one person distinguishable from another. The way a person behaves, therefore, is dependent on both the immediate influences of the environment and the person's 'history'. Behaviour patterns develop from a system of reward and punishment. Throughout life behaviour is continually being rewarded (or reinforced), or it is being punished (or negatively reinforced). The stronger the reward the more difficult will it be to change behaviour.

In a sense personality is the basis of survival in the world. Attitudes, skills, likes, dislikes, image of self, are the roots of repeated behaviour which have created an identity in life—something which distinctively belongs to a person.

Temperament is another word often used when describing personality. People can be described by one or several words: warm, aloof, excitable, suspicious, thoughtful, humorous, relaxed; but there is a difference between *mood* and the temperamental disposition to behave in a consistent manner. The 'warm' person may have *moods* in which he is withdrawn from social contact, but primarily his temperamental disposition is to appear warm and responsive.

Some temperamental dispositions or 'traits' of personality can be measured by tests. Given their validity, such tests (when supported by interview data) can provide important information about a person's suitability for various tasks and environments. Once again, the inherited, innate, constitutional, and environmental influences are jointly responsible for developing such temperamental dispositions.

Much of the basic formation of the personality occurs in the first six or seven years of life, but substantial readjustments may occur at certain points in the development of an individual, when first starting school, for instance, and with the onset of adolescence. Indeed the temperament is modified throughout life both by the notion of constitutional factors, like ageing, and by the process of continuous adjustment to the environment (learning). Cattell[1] notes that the capacity to handle emotional problems and 'subordinate impulses to more remote satisfactions increases steadily as people get older'.

Logically there should be no positive or negative value associated with personality traits, although people do tend to evaluate them. People have 'stock attitudes' to certain types, and to this extent 'stereotypes' of people are frequently used by others, for example stereotypes of the marketing man or the accountant. People usually look for traits in others which they expect to see in order to fit their stereotypes. This clouds a person's capacity to see people as they really are, and forms the basis of bias, misunderstanding, and poor communication.

Knowledge of the personality traits which an individual possesses can help in assessing his suitability for a given job and environment. It is possible to obtain 'profiles' of various combinations and strengths of an individual's traits which can be matched (along with other abilities and aptitudes) with the known requirements of a job. Such measuring of traits should only be carried out, and the results interpreted, by skilled and *experienced* personnel.

(b) Intelligence

Intelligence refers to the capacity which an individual has to deal with his environment in a logical, rational way. It is concerned with reasoning power, mechanical and spatial comprehension, speed and accuracy, verbal facility, and other factors. Performances on these different dimensions are frquently related, and it is possible to infer a general ability, an intellectual power, which can be applied to a wide range of problems. But differences do exist, and they are important. Intelligence tests are often applied to separate, for instance, an individual's verbal and numerical reasoning abilities, since facility with either or both may be important requirements in a job.

Different jobs require different levels of intellectual ability. A poor match between the demands of the job and the abilities of the individual can be costly for a company and harmful for the individual. In routine, repetitive work, more able people may become bored quickly, with a consequent deterioration in performance. Inability to keep up with the intellectual demands of a job may cause an individual to feel a failure and to show signs of stress and anxiety, again with associated effects on performance.

Two important aspects of intelligence, not easily assessed, are judgement and creativity. Judgement is demonstrated by the realistic assessment of people and situations, and by the production of workable solutions to problems. It may involve aspects of personality, such as emotional make up and social skills, but sound judgement, or lack of it, can often be detected in a candidate's employment record or in certain of his decisions. Creativity is demonstrated in an ability to see situations from a novel viewpoint, to propose insightful and possibly unconventional solutions to problems, and to initiate new ventures. Creativity is not necessarily associated with an unconventional trend or mode of life.

19

(c) Aptitude

As with intelligence, aptitude is concerned with the way in which a person deals with his environment, this time in a particular or exceptional way. An aptitude is a special skill, ability or 'flair'. Usually this appears to be inherited but it can be improved by training. Some aptitudes are related closely with intelligence, others are not. They cover a wide range—from mechanical aptitude to a flair for dealing with people; from a facility for dealing with numbers to a 'sense' of colour and design. Tests of various kinds exist to identify certain aptitudes and are of considerable value in selection and training. Interest however is very important. An aptitude is difficult to exploit if the person possessing it does not wish to use it. When a highly developed aptitude is combined with a strong interest, the result is often impressive.

(d) Attitudes

Much of life consists of perceiving things and evaluating them—that is, forming a negative or positive feeling towards them. Such evaluation is subsequently reflected in the nature of the behaviour displayed towards events and people. Some attitudes are so deep-rooted that the assumptions on which they are based are not questioned. Early in life, attitudes towards major areas of experience are developed, and these form a frame of reference by which behaviour in general is often judged. Having feelings for and against a whole range of social phenomena and people helps individuals to locate themselves in the world. Attitudes underline the what, how, and why of behaviour, and, supported by beliefs, become a relatively consistent influence and hence a cause of regularity in behaviour. Nonetheless, attitudes do change, and such change is part of the process of learning.

Some attitudes are changed because information and knowledge show that an attitude held was unreasonable. Many managers may have strong negative feelings about behavioural scientists—they are 'impractical', 'idealistic', etc. Such feelings would markedly affect any attempts at constructive discussion about human problems at work, because attitudes affect perspectives, and hence what is seen and heard. But learning about the research and theories of behavioural science through management education changes attitudes. Indeed, education is partly a process of changing attitudes through information exchange: changing by increasing knowledge. Within a company, attitudes about trade unions, other functions in the business, the shop-floor, authority, discipline, the product, the company, loyalty, and similar aspects of people and behaviour, are universal. People who share attitudes group together, and, to some extent, knowing what attitudes are in one or two areas makes it possible to predict what they will be in others, since there are traits with which it would be expected certain attitudes to be associated.

Changing attitudes is not simply a matter of providing rational information to show that an attitude is untenable: it is known that frequently such rational information is rejected in order to retain an attitude.

In looking at the individual, we can see that his identity consists of a number of aspects. These are:

PERSONALITY
INTELLIGENCE
APTITUDES
ATTITUDES (values and beliefs)
EXPERIENCE and MEMORY
KNOWLEDGE and SKILLS

Some of these are less open to change than others. At the 'core' of any individual there lie basic characteristics such as personality and intelligence, which in adult life are difficult to change, even if justification could be found for doing so. However, other aspects are open to change. Some aptitudes may be discovered and developed; attitudes, the interpretation of experience, and knowledge and skills may be changed and developed. It is these 'peripheral' aspects of identity which training seeks to change.

THE
INDIVIDUAL
AND ROLE

An individual does not behave as an isolated organism—he can only express himself within the context of others. His relationships with others are determined by a complicated system of rules and customs, which are largely unconscious in their execution. Society exists, and behaviour is regulated, because there are patterns of expected behaviour, conformity to which is ensured to a large degree either by external sanctions or by an individual's 'internalized' need to behave in certain ways. These patterns of expected behaviour are called ROLES. All people play numerous roles in life (husband, father, son, client manager, boss, subordinate, neighbour, friend), which require certain specific behaviour patterns if they are to be discharged successfully, and by so doing acquire the social approval and reward which accompanies successful behaviour. The demands of one role often conflict with those of another. A person playing the managerial role may well be obliged to work long hours, postpone holidays and perhaps be away from home frequently, and this conflicts with his roles of husband and parent. At work, instances may be found where 'moral' obligations to subordinates cannot be discharged by a manager if he is to play the role of managing an organization with obligations to act in the name of its survival and profitability. Redundancy measures create these strains for many managers. Role conflict also occurs between present and past roles, when for example a man has been promoted from shop floor to first line management, or from representative to sales manager.

Role is a useful concept. It focuses attention on the fact that there are behaviour patterns which exist independently of the personality. While different individuals will interpret the expected behaviour-pattern in different ways, the role will, in part at least, constrain an individual to behave according to the expectations of others.

In studying the behaviour of an individual, awareness is needed of the role he is attempting to play.

> How does he *perceive* the role?
> What role has he been *offered*?
> Does the role *conflict* with others?
> Has he the *ability* to play the role?

Some roles are loosely defined and hence more 'permissive' than others. These roles give an individual scope for interpretation, and to stamp his personality on it. Indeed such roles provide the opportunity for individuality. Other roles, for example, airline pilot, and many industrial roles, both managerial and shop-floor, provide little scope for interpretation. Job descriptions, rules, training, and the plant and equipment itself limit the degree of interpretation possible and often narrowly define the range of behaviour permissible.

GROUPS

A group consists of a number of people who co-operate in the pursuit of a common objective or task, and who are aware of a group identity and 'boundary'. Groups are systems of roles which are interdependent and may be formally defined—as in the case of a work group—or informally developed, as in a friendship group. The degree of formality in a group is indicated by the extent to which the relationship between individuals are ROLE relationships or PERSONAL relationships, e.g.

ROLE ⟷	PERSONAL
formal	informal
instrumental	affective
relationships	relationships

All groups control to some extent the individual member's behaviour by the social pressures which it exerts on the individual's interpretation of the role. The group's final sanction is the rejection of the individual, but it also exerts social pressure by withdrawing social approval, status rewards, and other socio-emotional aspects of structure or process. Structure refers to the arrangement of roles, for example the division of labour, the authority and status system, the group's size, and possibly, sub-groupings. Process is used as a term to describe the ongoing activities within a group: communication, emergence of leadership, the development of relationships, pairing, dependency, conflict, etc.

ORGANIZATION

An organization is an arrangement of human and physical resources for the purposes of carrying out transactions with the environment in such a manner that it ensures the survival of that organization. Organization is founded upon the need to control and integrate the activities of individuals and groups in the achievement of a task. The formal rules and procedures of any organization, which ensure a minimum level of integration of specialized and separated activities, require authority, that is, legitimate power vested in roles (offices), in order to ensure that the rules and procedures are observed. These formal rules and procedures would not be sufficient in themselves (or, if they were, would be too encyclopaedic and cumbersome) to ensure the successful operation of an organization. Values (commonly held beliefs) and attitudes, informal roles and procedures develop which make it possible for the organization to operate flexibly. However, not all informal aspects of organization may support the formal roles and procedures, and informal working arrangements may run contrary to the requirements of task achievement.

AUTHORITY

In any group or organization a structure of power relationships (pecking-order) can be observed. In organizations, authority is essentially the legitimate power to control and influence the behaviour of others and the use of resources. It exists because co-ordination requires decisions to be made and conflicts to be resolved. Every individual has a boss, and he must therefore learn to manage differences in status and power. Different personality types respond to being in authority, and being subject to it, in differing ways. Behavioural scientists have carried out research into the use of authority, since the manner in which it is exercised is known to influence an individual's motivation and performance.

CONFLICT   Research shows that conflict—disagreement leading to a power struggle—can be described as functional or dysfunctional (good or bad), depending on the point of view which is taken and on the short term/long term implications for the parties involved. Strikes—the classic expression of conflict—which prevent management from manufacturing goods for which there is a customer, may be described in the short term as dysfunctional for the organization. If, however, such disputes act as pressure upon management to introduce mechanization and automation, or to improve the representation and communications systems, with subsequent benefits in efficiency—then such conflict could be considered functional. Short term gains by local unions could have long term disadvantages for its members, if as a result, there was a reduction in employment choice. All people accept some form of authority, that is influence, which controls their behaviour. Conflict arises when individuals or groups, indeed organizations, no longer wholly accept as legitimate the control to which they are subject—the control which makes decisions for them, or resolves conflict between two parties.

Conflict in the past has been considered 'unhealthy'. Utopian views of organization and society have visualized conditions of total harmony. However, conflict can be functional, and is undoubtedly a part of the reality of collective and creative existence. The ability to manage conflict is an important managerial skill. The problem is mainly one of dealing openly with conflict, rather than repressing it. But repressing conflict is a characteristic of institutions which judge conflict to be undesirable and is likely to be associated with the inhibition of creativity and risk taking.

ALIENATION   Alienation occurs when certain needs are not fulfilled. If western society as a whole is looked at and compared with the needs of the individual as described by Maslow[2] it can be seen that by and large people's 'lower' order needs of warmth, food, and shelter, are being met.

When these needs are met adequately, people need fulfilment at the higher' levels, which if not met leads to the phenomenon of alienation. Boring, dull, and routine work is still common, and while tolerated when those employed in it were on the 'breadline', it may now be becoming intolerable. Some manifestations of alienation from work are:

(1) Withdrawal—'switching off'—particularly at the routine operative level, but not only in blue-collar jobs. Many

people go to their work place but withdraw from activity until the day is over. One man, asked what he thought about while he was working, said, 'I don't wake up until the end of the shift. The day begins for me at 5 o'clock'. Thus one aspect of alienation is when the work content is so boring and dull and provides no 'food' for the individual's self-esteem (central to image of self), that individuals withdraw from work mentally and, increasingly, bodily.

(2) Aggressive attitudes, which are common among workers who have alienating jobs. Militant trades unions are formed, complaints and arguments with management arise (demarcation disputes, go-slows, unofficial strikes, absenteeism) over apparently minor details.

The effects of alienating work on non-work activities are not clearly understood. Some people believe that a dull and boring job leads to a dull and boring life, others believe the opposite. There is evidence to suggest that, according to personality type, both apply.

Alienation is associated with the feeling of powerlessness. This leads to a disinclination to be concerned with, or to participate in, the affairs of organizations and institutions, the character of which shape society.

PARTICIPATION

Participation means an increase in the amount of involvement which people have in the work they do; the extent to which they can take part in what they do. Participation really refers to the 'amount' of any individual which is actively taking part in a job. In the example of an alienated workman, only a very small 'part' of him was concerned with the job, a large part—the thinking conscious part—was somewhere else, daydreaming or sleeping. Participation is an attempt to engage more of an individual, believing that this will meet some of his higher level needs—the needs for self-expression and self-fulfilment.

In the work situation, participation is often manifested in terms of the control which a man will have over the content of his work. A man will be participating if he has, for example, a greater say in the way he organizes his work and in the range of tasks which he is required to carry out.

Some experts have seen the growth of various forms of participation (worker representatives on the Board, Joint Consultation, dispersal of power and authority within the organization, etc.) as essential to the running of complex industrial societies.

The following chapters discuss in greater detail many of these concepts, and some of the techniques which have been developed out of the growing knowledge about them.

REFERENCES

(1) Cattell, R. B., *The scientific analysis of personality*, Harmondsworth: Penguin, 1965.

(2) Maslow, A. H., 'A theory of human motivation'. In H. J. Leavitt and L. P. Pondy, *Readings in managerial psychology*, Chicago: University of Chicago Press, 1964, pp. 6-24.

4

The changing relationship between man and work

This chapter covers briefly the ways in which the relationship between man and work has been looked at over the years, and pays particular attention to the present-day view. A central theme is that of motivation: what motivates people to work, and what can be done to motivate them to work more effectively. Management is besieged with ideas for obtaining higher productivity from employees at all levels profit sharing, stock options, productivity bargaining, industrial training, group working, music-while-you-work, new selection methods, different colour schemes for work rooms, take-home booklets, industrial democracy, human relations training, changing leadership styles, work simplification, job enlargement, incentive schemes, job rotation, and more recently, job enrichment. These and other techniques, however different from each other they may appear, are aimed at the relationship between the employee and his work. They seek fundamentally to influence the feelings a person has towards his work in such a way that work effort is sustained or improved. All these approaches have been tried, but they are incomplete in themselves for resolving the problem of man's effort at work. Indeed it is unlikely that completely effective working situations will ever be obtained. Management will always be concerned with balancing employees' requirements against the needs of the organization. However, some of the needs of the organization are not as incompatible with the needs of the employee, as has been thought in the past.

The man/work relationship is governed by what makes the man work—what motivates him. Motives are needs, wants and drives within the individual which find release through the acquisition of some experience or object from the environment. The goal sought will not be wanted for its own sake, but for the reward, satisfaction and the release from the tension of being motivated. This very simple description might imply that motives come one at a time, are conscious and always directing behaviour to a goal clearly obtainable in the immediate future. In fact few motives are

27

quite so singular in their effect on behaviour. Motivating forces are often unconscious, interacting, and dependent to a large degree on what the environment is presenting as a stimulus.

There is a reason for everything that people do, although these reasons are not always apparent. Even when it is believed that the needs being satisfied are known ('I am buying this car because it's economical and its finish is excellent . . .') there will undoubtedly be other motives which have influenced the decision processes, of which an individual will be partially, or possibly wholly, unaware. People give reasons for their actions which are often rationaliz-ations, that is, cognitive reasons. Such reasons are more acceptable than the true motivation. The problem of researching into the reasons why people work, and the satisfaction they gain, suffers from this, for the true motivation (that which causes the behaviour) will be hidden behind rationalization. It may be more acceptable to say that one works to have responsibility and to be of service, than to recognize the primacy of job security, pay, and pension rights.

With these thoughts in mind concerning motivation, it is interesting to look at the changes in the way the man/work relationship has been managed over the years.

SIGNIFICANT CHANGES IN THE MAN/WORK RELATIONSHIP
Before the Industrial Revolution (up to about 1770)

The relationship between man and work was substantially different before the industrial revolution from what it is today. Society at that time was not accustomed to rapid change, and possessed a social structure which was considerably more inflexible than it is now. This manifested itself in, for example, people pursuing a way of life which did not change from generation to generation. To state what a person did for a living usually gave a clear indication of not only his occupation but the life he led: the type of house he lived in, his 'style' of living, the types of people whom his children would marry. Work was as integral a part of a man's life as every other aspect of his living.

A further significant difference was that work to a large extent was self-pacing and consisted of 'whole tasks'. A carpenter, in addition to making things (and possibly selling them) would also be concerned with providing himself with all the raw materials— including cutting down trees.

The Industrial Revolution (from 1770 to about 1840)

The industrial revolution saw considerable changes in society. Developments in technology led to ways of making products which people needed on a scale never before envisaged in the history of man. Many machines were put together under one roof—in a 'manufactory'—and people were brought in to work them. For the first time people in great numbers were confronted with work the nature of which was mostly generated by the machines rather than by themselves. Men became machine-paced rather than self-paced. The bringing together of people to work in factories had a severely dislocating effect on the stable society. The sense of order, balance, and security was swept aside in a few years. The countryside was abandoned for the towns, and people found themselves living in increasingly large communities without any sense of 'place' which they had previously had. There was large-scale social disorientation, with the associated upheavals and disturbances in society, and physical and psychological trauma and hardship for the individual. The creation of wealth became a preoccupation of the economy and little or no consideration was given to people's needs. Indeed, people were present just as were the machines and the materials in order to facilitate this creation of wealth. People were treated as machines and materials, to be used when required with a minimum of maintenance, and rejected if not effective. All this gave rise to the social evils of that time: exploitation, disease, hunger, and poor housing.

Slowly steps were taken to alleviate what had become appalling conditions for the people who were busily creating the wealth. Reforms were instituted, with legislation being passed in Parliament on hours of work, minimum age of employment, working conditions, care for the destitute, provision for education, political representation, etc. By present standards these moves were minimal but they did represent a very significant and important start.

Social Reform (from 1840 to about 1910)

The 'scientific' approach to management was a logical and rational one. Logic and rationality had been so successful in unlocking nature's secrets that a similar approach to man at work seemed 'logical'. The emphasis was on making people work more effectively by breaking down large tasks into smaller units, by clearly defining the way a task should be done, and by specifying how long it should take. People were then required to do the task in the right way and at the right speed, over and over again. People in fact were required to behave as machines. To make sure this happened, performance was measured, incentives were applied to reinforce conforming behaviour, and penalties applied for non-conformity.

Scientific Management (from 1910 to about 1940)

> ... man's role was concerned to be only that of an element or cog in a complex production system dominated by costly equipment. In mechanical systems, elements must be completely designed if they are to function when transposed. This

29

requirement states that initiative and self-organization are not acceptable for they may increase both system variability and the risk of failure.[1]

Gilbreth[2] and Taylor[3] sum up this machine approach to man at work. At this stage in the development of industrial society, 'material stimulants' to productive effort were assumed to be the primary force operating on the employee at work. Taylor's work was undertaken with the major motivational assumption of 'economic/rational' man, an assumption which saw man's performance as limited by physiological fatigue and enhanced by economic incentives. Methods to simplify and specialize work, and payment by results (piece-work), were the techniques of scientific management. Paradoxically Taylor's work on methods, which resulted in simplification of work, and the increasing use of mechanization, had the consequence of reducing the incentive effects of payment. The reduced importance of wages in work motivation which is often reported, may not simply be a function of change in values and attitudes but of real changes in the opportunities for the employee individually to influence to any degree the size of his wage packet.

The inadequacy of mechanical perceptions of economic-rational man led to the development of what has been called 'welfare capitalism'. Companies attempted to associate workers with the organization by the provision of facilities and conditions which, it was hoped, both attracted and retained the worker. The point of focus in attempts to motivate the work force was the environment which surrounded a job.

The Hawthorne Studies—the Human Relations Approach (1924 to 1931)

Probably the first step in understanding more about what motivated people at work took place in the USA in the 'twenties, in what is now known as the Hawthorne experiment. A full account of this very significant work is given by Roethlisberger and Dickson[4]. This study was carried out at the Hawthorne works of the Western Electric Company, near Chicago. There were some 29,000 people employed at the plant in the manufacture of telephone equipment for much of the USA. The management of this company was concerned with the problems of identifying the factors which affected performance at work, and they obtained outside help to do this from the National Research Council of the National Academy of Sciences. The research group, headed by Elton Mayo, consisted of people from both the research council and the company, and was located organizationally in the industrial relations department.

The study at its outset was concerned with finding out in much greater detail what sorts of physical conditions affected work. Preliminary investigations (lasting from 1924 to 1927) primarily into the effects of the level of lighting on work, found very little correlation between output and brightness. This led to a broadening of the original investigations into an examination of other physical conditions (e.g. effects of rest pauses), and also an investigation of employee's attitudes. Examination of the physical conditions was carried out with a group of girls who were concerned with the assembly of telephone relays. A large number of girls were employed in this fairly routine operation in the plant, and in order to be able to study the effects of the physical conditions more easily, a small number of this larger group was placed in a separate room away from the main work group. This group of six girls was then left to carry on with the job but with an observer present in the room in order to record what was happening. Considerable pains were taken to record actual output, as accurate production figures were crucial.

Soon after the group began working as a separate unit, various changes took place in length of hours worked, in times of starting and finishing, in the number of rest pauses the girls had, together with a strict control for some of the time over what the girls ate during their working hours—their food being provided by the company and being carefully noted.

The most significant finding out of this study (which lasted from April 1927 to June 1929) was that despite the various changes which went on in the physical conditions of work, output steadily increased. The changes that were made were both objectively positive and negative at various times, but even so output improved. This phenomenon is now known as the 'Hawthorne effect' and since then it has been satisfactorily explained. The girls in the relay assembly test room (as it was called) responded to the Hawthorne effect rather than all the other things the investigators were doing—in that they were responding to being a group of people identified for a study, and given either implicitly or explicitly special treatment. These girls were separated from the main body of relay assemblers; they were given, relatively speaking, better working conditions than the main group, and they were involved in what was happening in that they were informed of the changes that were taking place and indeed had a chance to discuss them with the researchers. Furthermore, the researchers themselves were, without realizing it, guilty of biasing the results. When one of the girls in the group became increasingly unco-operative about the changes that were periodically being made it was decided to remove her and bring in someone else.

31

Arising from the questions which the relay assembly experiment raised, and also because of more general concerns about employees' views, an enquiry into employees' attitudes began in 1928. An interviewing programme was undertaken with the aim of talking to everyone who worked at the Hawthorne plant. In the event, some 21,000 people were interviewed between 1928 and 1930. The interviews—which were carried out by employees—were initially 30 minute structured events, but later they became unstructured and lasted for usually 90 minutes. The aim was to obtain an appreciation of what the employees thought about their jobs, their supervision, their working conditions, etc. A wealth of material was gathered and broadly analysed into favourable and unfavourable comments (there were twice as many unfavourable as there were favourable comments). The material formed the basis of many changes in the company, especially in people's working conditions, and it was also used as a basis for supervisory training courses. The material also suggested that sociological factors were important to people at work. Relationships with people emerged as a significant theme, and arising partly from these data, a further study was considered, and this one was a deliberate sociological investigation.

'Bank wiring' was the task which was chosen for this study. Fourteen men were told to move into a room away from their bank wiring colleagues so that they could be observed. The observer was explained to be completely neutral (as in fact he turned out to be). Apart from being isolated there were few differences between the 'Bank Wiring Observation Group' and the other bank wirers. These differences were that all of the group members were interviewed three times during the 'life' of the group (which was seven months) about their attitudes to work; they were all physically examined; and were all tested for ability and aptitude in order to explore any relation between ability and/or aptitude and performance (in the event there was none).

Output varied little during the life of the group. The men quickly settled on a fixed rate of work which was about 85 percent of the company 'bogey' or target. Group rules quickly developed. Operators exceeding the group's production norm were called 'ratebusters', those producing too little were known as 'chiselers', those who 'told' on colleagues were 'squealers'. Although there was an organizational hierarchy in the group of fourteen men (there were two inspectors who were senior to the others), the group norm was one of the minimum social distance. An inspector was not allowed to behave any differently from the others, apart of course from doing his job. A system of punishing transgressors, known as 'binging' , developed. This consisted of punching someone quite hard on the upper arm. Binging became a very important mechanism for controlling conflict in the group, for example two men who were fiercely arguing were told to 'bing and make up'.

A variable work pattern was recorded in this group. Although daily output was constant some people would work hard early in the day and then ease up, whilst others would do the opposite. Territorial issues became important, as the group of fourteen soon differentiated into two groups of six and four. The group of four resisted the continued leadership bids from one of the remaining four 'isolates'. Another isolate was firmly rejected by both groups as he was a persistent squealer. Of the two definable groups the larger one was much more rebellious and anti-establishment than the smaller.

There have been a number of reinterpretations of the Hawthorne studies. Recently Paul Blumberg[5] has re-examined the data and conclusions of the relay assembly test room investigations contained in Roethlisberger and Dickson[4] and has argued that the effects of the participation of the girls in decision-making about their work was virtually ignored as a factor in the reasons for increased production. His argument is supported by accumulated evidence on the effects on motivation of the worker being allowed more control over work methods and work pace.

The Hawthorne studies were a very important development in the understanding of the relationship between man and his work. They symbolized the move from the traditional view of 'mechanistic' man, to a more progressive view of 'organic' man, whose motivations were much more complex than hitherto had been realized. The painstakingly gathered data has proved to be of immense value and it has been used time and time again as a reference point for other studies, and for theorizing.

The Hawthorne investigations lasted from 1924-1931, and ended because of the depression. Their value is a tribute to the considerable faith and efforts of the company and the researchers.

Since the Hawthorne studies, the relationship between man and work has been investigated further, and what is now emerging is a more complex view of motivation. One of the most important contributors to this more sophisticated approach is Maslow[6].

Maslow's hypothetical 'hierarchy of needs' proposes a dynamic conception of man's motivation, one that is able to take into account both personality variables and the process of social change.

THE PRESENT VIEW OF MOTIVATION
Abraham Maslow

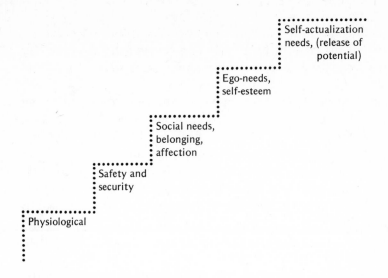

Fig. 4.1 *Maslow's hierarchy of needs*

The hierarchy of needs model was the result of Maslow's clinical studies, from which he generalized a classification of at least five sets of goals, which he called man's basic needs. (See Fig. 4.1)

The need at each level has to be satisfied before the need at the next higher level is activated. Until the body has provided for its fundamental survival needs, it will not seek safety and security, and until these are themselves satisfied, social needs will not become a motivating force.

Physiological Needs

Man's need for food, rest and exercise, is obvious. At its most basic level there is the body's need to maintain automatically a constantly normal state of the bloodstream. The body seeks 'homeostasis', that is physiological balance and equilibrium. However, the consummatory behaviour involved in meeting physiological needs serve as a means of satisfying other higher level needs as well. For example a person who is feeling hungry may actually be seeking comfort and dependence rather than protein. Of course physiological needs are not the sole motivating forces for higher level needs. Primary needs, however, will be more potent motivators in circumstances of physiological deprivation. 'A person who is lacking food, safety, love and esteem would, most probably, hunger for food more strongly than for anything else.'[7] Furthermore, being dominated by one need will change an individual's perceptions. For the hungry man, utopia is a place with plenty of food, for those starved of affection, utopia is a place full of easy strong relationships.

34

When the desire for food and other physiological necessities is satisfied, other 'higher' needs emerge, and these then dominate the organism. People have a need to be free from danger, threat and other general privations of life. Freedom from others' arbitrary action is required, and this need for security is the point at which man co-operates with others in order to ensure predictable behaviour. Security needs are not only concerned with basic physical security; in modern industrial society security may mean having protection from the arbitrary actions of employers, having some notion of a desirable future, 'social' security, and some measure of protection from the vicissitudes of employment and health.

Safety and Security Needs

If the above needs are met then there will emerge the love, affection and belonging needs. A person is likely to feel the absence of friends, and of family, and will seek to develop affectionate, warm and emotionally supportive relationships. The need for these relationships will lend weight to a group's pressure for conformity, and in seeking to satisfy these social needs the individual is likely to forego the higher level needs of ego-expression and self-esteem. To be able to meet needs for social intercourse, forms of self-expression which might be disruptive within the group, are sacrificed. Belonging therefore also means giving up something. Norms and codes are sources of rejection by the groups to which people belong.

Social Needs

> All people . . . have a need or desire for a stable, firmly based, usually high evaluation of themselves, for self-respect, or self-esteem, and for the esteem of others. (Maslow)

The Ego, or Esteem, Needs

The need for self-esteem arises from a requirement not to feel weak, helpless and inferior. The satisfaction of self-esteem needs gives rise to feelings of confidence, of worth, of strength, and capability, of being useful and necessary. Thus the opportunity to behave in ways which bring the esteem of others, and generates respect of self, is vitally important. The role of work, the self-esteem to be derived from one's feelings about one's work, and from the evaluation of it by others in the satisfaction of this need, is, in industrial society, especially predominant. The status of the work done, its 'social' evaluation, is only one part of the fulfilment of esteem needs however. Earnings derived from work over and above basic requirements (discretionary income), are used to purchase things and services and opportunities which are also a source of esteem (by various social groupings). There are, of course, many other means by which self-esteem is derived. The essential thing is that man has a 'self-image', and he needs facilities and opportunities to behave in ways which result in positive reinforcement about his 'self-image' from others.

Self Actualization Needs

Even when all other needs are satisfied, Maslow states that a new discontent and restlessness may emerge: 'What a man C A N be, he M U S T be.' The tendency towards self-actualization, or self-fulfilment, emerges only when other lower order needs have been satisfied. What form self-actualization will take is enormously variable, but the process can be thought of as deriving from the need to grow psychologically, to attain a degree of autonomy and choice about self, and to release potential.

While Maslow's 'hierarchy of needs' model is often interpreted as if the hierarchy were in a fixed order, it is not nearly as rigid as many have implied. Maslow notes that, from his experience, there are some people for whom self-esteem seems more important than love, although clinically he interprets this as 'seeking self-esteem for the sake of love rather than for self-esteem itself'. In certain people the level of aspiration may be lowered—the need for security may come to dominate the life of an individual. Indeed many people have a need for love, membership and belonging, which is sufficiently strong as to permanently 'lower' their levels of aspiration.

The concept of self-actualization, which has become a cliché, bandied around to 'explain' all manner of industrial phenomena, is not an easy one to understand. 'It refers to the desire for self-fulfilment, namely to the tendency for one to become actualized in what one is potentially'. (Maslow)

Maslow's model of the basic needs of man has had an important effect on considerations of man and work. It has served to focus attention on the higher level need satisfaction which can be derived from work. More than the human relations movement it has acted as a counter-weight to the demands of the industrial engineer to de-skill and simplify work, for it has resulted in attention being paid not only to the physical and social environment in which a job is done, but also to the actual content of the work itself, since it is only through performance in a task that satisfaction of the higher level needs may be obtained at work.

While there may be academic debate as to the innate or learned nature of these growth-fulfilment needs, it is clear that industrial society brought about tremendous changes in education, communication, mobility, etc. which may have provided the cultural pressures and opportunities, at least for a proportion of the population, to 'self-actualize'. It is interesting to note that

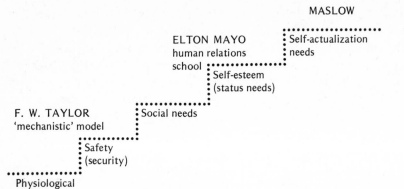

Fig. 4.2 *Maslow's hierarchy and the changing approach to man's work needs*

Maslow's hierarchy also expresses to some degree the direction of social change. From an historical point of view, the different assumptions about motivation are probably a consequence of social change itself, since new conditions have acted as a stimulus, which motivate laymen and scientists alike to find new explanations for new phenomena.

The changing approach to man's needs at work (and hence to his motivation) can be generalized by reference to Maslow's hierarchy of needs. (See Fig. 4.2)

Currently, motivation is regarded as a complex issue. From 'economic-man' through 'social man', to 'self-actualizing' man, it is now possible to recognize 'complex man'. In his book, *Work and Motivation*[8], in which he reviewed well over 500 research investigations, Vroom states that there is no single theory which encompasses all the research data; and that 'Effective and ineffective performance may have affective consequences per se; the magnitude of these consequences is a function of the nature of the task, the "personality" of the worker, and their interrelation.'

While no single theory may be forthcoming, there are a number of theories which have resulted in practical attempts to change work in such a way that it met the needs of employees to a fuller extent. It is appropriate to describe here the motivational theories on which these analytical and change techniques are based although, in chapter 10, the practice will be examined under the heading of 'job design'.

The work of Professor Frederick Herzberg is most frequently referred to in terms of the technique of 'job enrichment' which has resulted from his theory of motivation. In the late 1950's, Herzberg and a number of colleagues embarked on a study to

Frederick Herzberg

attempt to resolve the many contradictions which were evident in the findings of industrial psychologists in their research into work and motivation. The researchers asked people to describe in detail what was occurring in their jobs at times when they had felt unusually satisfied, interested or enthusiastic about their work, and similarly for times when they had felt unusually dissatisfied, frustrated or unhappy. The initial investigation was carried out among engineers and accountants, and the results were published in the book *The Motivation to Work*[9].

The study indicated that factors which were associated with satisfaction were different in kind from those associated with dissatisfaction. Satisfaction and dissatisfaction, it was concluded, were not simple opposites, rather they tended to have their source in different aspects of the work situation, and the removal of a dissatisfying factor from work would not have the often assumed effect of creating job satisfaction. Herzberg himself came to call the theory of motivation which recognized the differences between factors which satisfy and those which dissatisfy, the MOTIVA-TION/HYGIENE theory. A comparison of the satisfactions and dissatisfactions for accountants and engineers—Herzberg's original study—is shown below. (Fig. 4.3)

Since this work the research has been replicated many times. Its population sample covers many different nationalities (including Britain) ages, educational backgrounds, types of job, and levels of seniority. The findings are, on the whole, very consistent, and the 'verification of the theory' is contained in a later book by Herzberg called *Work and the Nature of Man*[10].

The Motivation/Hygiene theory has drawn attention to the inadequacy of previous management assumptions about work and motivation, which have often been aimed at increasing worker satisfaction by removing those factors in the surroundings of the job about which the employee may have expressed dissatisfaction. It has been in part management's assumption that job satisfaction leads to good performance; Herzberg and his associates have reversed this assumption, and indicated that it is more likely that good performance leads to job satisfaction, a conclusion that is supported by reference both to Herzberg's theory, and to Maslow's higher level needs. The higher level needs cannot be met unless the characteristics of tasks are changed to provide opportunity for autonomy, the use of skills and abilities and expression of potential—all elements in self-actualization. Logically also it is unlikely, unless some mediating influence such as ego-satisfactions can be hypothesized, that job satisfaction leads to the motivation to work.

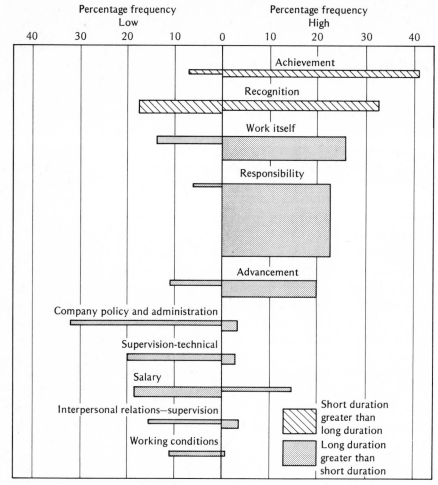

Fig. 4.3 *Comparison of satisfiers and dissatisfiers*

A motivated person was defined earlier as one who has an unsatisfied need; it is difficult, therefore, to understand how the creation of job satisfaction results in motivation, unless it is hypothesized that such satisfaction induces in the worker a state of mind which recognizes the increased value of the work role to the individual. Vroom[8], in a discussion of the relationship between job satisfaction and job performance, notes:

> Individuals are satisfied with their jobs to the extent to which the job provides them with what they desire and they perform effectively in them to the extent that effective performance leads to the attainment of what they desire.

While job satisfaction and job performance must be considered as conceptually and empirically separate outcomes of the person-role relationship, Vroom's conclusion is in line with Herzberg's basic thesis, that good job performance leads to job satisfaction, for which Vroom reports there is more evidence. However, all depends in this case on what the individual desires. Herzberg's theory generalizes for all classes of individual—and indeed his theories (where they have been applied and reported on) receive considerable validation in experimental situations. But it does fail to take into account personality variables and the individual's orientation to work, and these will obviously have a marked effect on the nature of the satisfaction a person desires from work. There are studies which are a challenge to Herzberg's two-factor theory. Walker and Guest[11] reported opposite findings. In this study, workers were most satisfied with pay and security factors, while dissatisfaction was for them located in job-content factors—the pacing of the work by the assembly line.

There are further problems with the Motivation/Hygiene theory. That is, there may be a tendency to ascribe dissatisfaction to those factors which represent the management and administration of the organization, rather than to name those things which reflect in part at least on the individual's self-esteem (e.g., lack of recognition, of responsibility, and achievement). Secondly, Herzberg's theory depends upon a relationship between job satisfaction and job-performance, and often there is a marked absence of consistent correlation. In a summary of factors which are associated with job satisfaction in a large number of studies, Vroom[8] gives a general picture of a satisfying work role. A work role which appears conducive to job satisfaction is one which provides:

(1) HIGH PAY
(2) SUBSTANTIAL PROMOTIONAL OPPORTUNITIES
(3) CONSIDERATE AND PARTICIPATIVE SUPERVISION
(4) OPPORTUNITIES TO INTERACT WITH PEERS
(5) VARIED DUTIES and
(6) HIGH DEGREE OF CONTROL OVER WORK METHOD AND WORK PACE

While some (6, 2 and possible 5) are linked with the Motivation/Hygiene theory, the remainder are in Herzberg's terms sources of dissatisfaction, rather than as reported by Vroom, important elements in job satisfaction. Furthermore, as Herzberg's findings do not take into account the individual's orientation to work, they are unable to explain the empirical possibility of having the following combination of satisfaction and performance attributes of a job. (See Fig. 4.4)

It is probable that in each of the boxes could be found, in the SAME job, different levels of satisfaction and performance explainable by reference to personality variables.

	High Satisfaction	Low Satisfaction
High Performance		
Low Performance		

Fig. 4.4

The work of the Tavistock Institute of Human Relations has been one of the major elements in the development of the behavioural sciences approaches to job and organization design. The concept of the socio-technical system[12] (see also chapter 6) has emphasized the need for job design to take into account not only factors associated with technical system efficiency, but also the needs of the social system, that is, the psycho/sociological needs of people at work. In a number of studies into organization design[13] and industrial democracy[14], the members of the Tavistock Institute have developed guidelines to the general psychological requirements that pertain to the content of a job. That it is possible to redesign jobs according to the following criteria rests upon the evidence that men have requirements of their work other than those usually specified in a contract of employment (i.e., other than wages, hours, safety, security of tenure, etc.). In part these needs refer to the higher level needs proposed by Maslow, and are (independently) undoubtedly related to the theories of Herzberg. The following list is taken from Emery and Thorsrud[14]:

The Tavistock Institute of Human Relations

(1) The need for the content of a job to be reasonably demanding of the worker in terms other than sheer endurance, and yet to provide (at least)* a minimum of variety (not necessarily novelty);

(2) the need for being able to learn on the job and to go on learning; again it is a question of neither too much nor too little;

(3) the need for (at least)* some minimal area of decision-making that the individual can call his own;

(4) the need for (at least)* some minimal degree of social support and recognition in the workplace;

(5) the need for the individual to be able to relate what he does and what he produces to his social life;

(6) the need to feel that the job leads to some sort of desirable future.

*Author's additions in parentheses.

These requirements are not confined to operators on the factory floor, nor is it possible to meet them in the same way in all work settings or for all kinds of people.

These requirements are too general at this point to serve as principles of job design; however, some expansion of these basic needs, linked to objective job characteristics will be undertaken in chapter 10 on Job Design.

CONCLUSIONS

While behavioural science is currently concerned with the complexity of factors associated with motivation and work, it is apparent that in general terms the major contemporary approach has been to redesign work in such a way that it permits increased job satisfactions to be derived from improved performance. Although it is reported in a number of instances that an increase in job satisfaction (through job enlargement and/or job enrichment) does not result in improved job performance, satisfaction is negatively related to turnover and absence. It seems therefore that an increase in job satisfaction by changing of INTRINSIC and/or EXTRINSIC factors (alternatively improving lower and/or higher order need satisfactions) may or may not lead to an increase in work performance, depending in large part upon the individual's characteristics, orientation to work, and upon the nature of the technology being worked. It appears likely, however, that the employee's relationship with the organization is positively affected, and results in the lowering of personnel and training costs.

All theories are generalizations and, hence, open to exception. It is the sign of a good theory that it is open to refutation, and yet is not brought tumbling down by the first objection, but provides a building block for further knowledge. The current position which has been arrived at in the consideration of work and motivation reflects a large number of causal influences affecting performance and satisfaction at work. Some measure of dissatisfaction may be felt because there is no one theory which simplifies the approach to job design and organization change, and that one is forced to deal with complexity, partial explanatory models, and each empirical situation. In the end the relationship between an *individual* and his work is being dealt with, and this relationship can be mediated by all manner of factors. Herbst[15] writes:

> I had started off with the expectation that it would be possible . . . to formulate a theory of behaviour applicable to all persons and groups. Examination of case after case obtained in the pupil-task study led to the abandonment of

this belief. It was not possible to find even a pair of children for whom the interrelationship of behaviour variables would be regarded as similar. It is true that if the data for a class of children are summed together, a stable pattern of relationships between behaviour variables emerges. However the results obtained this way bear no relation to the pattern of relationships found for any individual child. This leaves the problem of how data obtained by population-sample studies can be interpreted. The indications are that they refer to properties of populations but not necessarily to characteristics of individual human behaviour.

Returning to the original concepts of MOTIVATION and WORK the usefulness can be acknowledged of the theories and models in lending insight and ordering ideas on this matter. These concepts require consideration of motivation as a phenomenon which causes an individual to seek certain satisfactions, and which will vary with individual attributes and circumstances; and require consideration, also, of work as an activity which, in providing a range of relationships for the individual, gives opportunities to meet various types of needs and satisfactions.

The history of research into motivation and work is one which has passed through a number of phases in which a number of these relationships have been singled out for special attention in the attempt to improve productivity, effort, and satisfaction. Contemporary perspectives while adopting a more complex approach, have been concerned to examine the individual's relationship with his role, and to provide new stimulus to the individual by relating him more satisfyingly and effectively to work, through increased responsibility, decision-making, variety, autonomy, both as an individual and in the context of group work.

Projecting the present trend suggests that as people become better educated they will increasingly look for work which meets needs of a higher level. To deal with this it is very likely that a growth in organization and job design will occur. Production systems will not be designed on technical criteria alone, they will also embody social criteria in an attempt to meet both the needs of the technology and the needs of the people. The *content* of work will tend to engage more of the individual than it does at present, and for this to happen knowledge will have to increase in the area of individual and group needs, as well as in ways of coping with technologies to meet individual and group needs. As individuals, in their many roles, become more the focus of attention, so expertise concerning social interactions will increase.

As the trends toward fulfilling higher order needs from work continues, people will begin to ask questions concerning what this work is for. The significance of values will begin to emerge. On an increasing scale it is likely that people will not wish to work on activities which do not relate to aims which they have concerning the way they wish to spend their lives. This is already noticeable in the USA. In the space technology industry, for example, a considerable effort has been spent in developing a fulfilling organizational and job environment on which scientists and technologists can work, only to find that these gifted people, after some time, leave in order to spend their working time in the pursuit of helping other people. The purpose of work will be more and more questioned by those selling their services and some forms of work may become highly unpopular because of their nature and orientation.

Technical advances may make work as it is understood today less and less of a necessity. As a general trend hours at work will get shorter, and holidays will get longer. For some work as such will shift from the rather imperative character which it has at present, to an increasingly optional activity. Conventionally, work experience is thought of as determining the character of leisure time; it is more likely, as time passes, that the reverse will be true. As the world outside of work becomes an increasingly attractive alternative to going to work (let alone giving a good performance when there) management's strategy, assuming it wants able and interested employees, must be to make work an attractive alternative to leisure.

REFERENCES

(1) Davis, L. E., 'The design of jobs'. *Tavistock Institute of Human Relations, Doc.* No. T.736, 1965.
(2) Gilbreth, F. B., *Motion Study*, New York: Van Nostrand & Co., 1911.
(3) Taylor, F. W., *Scientific Management*, New York: Harper, 1911.
(4) Roethlisberger, F. J., and Dickson, W. J., *Management and the Worker*, Harvard University Press, 1939.
(5) Blumberg, P., *Industrial Democracy: the Sociology of Participation*, Constable, 1968.
(6) Maslow, A. H., *Motivation and Personality*, New York: Harper Row, 1954.
(7) Maslow, A. H., 'A theory of human motivation', in H. J. Leavitt and L. P. Pondy, *Readings in managerial psychology*, University of Chicago Press, 1964, pp. 6-24.

(8) Vroom, V. H., *Work and Motivation*, New York: Wiley, 1964.

(9) Herzberg, F., Mausner, B., and Snyderman, B., *The Motivation to Work*, New York: Wiley, 1959.

(10) Herzberg, F., *Work and the Nature of Man*, Cleveland and New York: World Publishing Co., 1966.

(11) Walker, C. R., and Guest, R. M. *The Man on the Assembly Line*, Harvard University Press, 1952.

(12) Emery, F. E., and Trist, E. L., 'Socio-technical systems'. In F. E. Emery (ed.) *Systems Thinking*, Penguin, 1969, pp. 281-296. See also: Emery, F. E., 'Characteristics of Socio-Technical Systems', *Tavistock Institute of Human Relations Doc.* No. 527, 1959.

(13) Trist, E. L., Higgin, G. W., Murray, H. and Pollock, A. B., *Organizational Choice: Capabilities of Groups at the Coal Face Under Changing Technologies.* London: Tavistock Publications, 1963; Rice, A. K., and Miller, E. J., *Systems of Organization*, Tavistock Publications, 1967; Rice, A. K., *Productivity and Social Organization: the Ahmedabad Experiment*, Tavistock Publications (Social Science Paperbacks), 1970.

(14) Emery, F. E., and Thorsrud, E. *Form and Content in Industrial Democracy*, Tavistock Publications, 1969.

(15) Herbst, P. G., *Behavioural Worlds: the Study of Single Cases*, Tavistock Publications, 1970.

5
Group behaviour

Much of an individual's behaviour is best understood in the context of his environment. This applies as much to the work situation, where the individual usually finds himself working with a group, as it does elsewhere. Although managers may express doubts about committees or project teams, group working and the control that groups exercise over individual behaviour is an important feature of organizational life. Groups are a point of identity for the individual and, in terms of the organization's objectives, can influence his behaviour positively or negatively. An individual's attitude towards production goals, leadership, tasks, and relationships with others, are all partly determined by the groups to which he belongs.

There is considerable management interest in the way groups behave. The focus of training, for example, is shifting from training the individual to training the group, and many training methods use the group as the learning unit. Concern with work groups, however, has a relatively long history, commencing with the human relations movement in early management theory. This concern has been incorporated in a broader approach and now continues in the field of organizational development and change. It now emphasizes the importance of the structure and the training of groups as the units of performance, change, and development.

WHAT IS A
GROUP?

A group consists of a number of people who have:

- a common objective or task,
- an awareness of a group identity and 'boundary',
- a minimum set of agreed values and norms, which regulates their relatively exclusive mutual interaction.

There is, however, no sharp dividing line between a group and a collection of individuals. The group is really limited by the opportunities for mutual interaction and awareness. Aggregates of people—a social class, a crowd, a large department—do not constitute a group even though the people may think of themselves as 'we'.

An industrial organization is made up of various groupings of employees. These groupings are a function of the requirements of the work (the division of labour and the technology), and of the social and psychological needs of its members. Apart from the minority, whose personality traits and/or work isolates them, work is for the most part at all levels accomplished in working groups. In any group and organization there is a continuous exchange relationship in operation between the individual and the group. For performing a function in a group the individual seeks rewards such as recognition, status, membership, social support and security. These kinds of reward are those which groups provide whether they be strictly work groups, or informal voluntary groups formed during work leisure periods. They often function to provide an individual with a sense of his own identity, which is an important psychological need. In exchange for the rewards, a member of a group will often deny himself certain other satisfactions in order to retain his membership and facilitate the cohesion of the group, for example he may work longer hours than he needs to if another group member is ill. Co-operativeness among members makes it possible to allocate roles, co-ordinate activities, and jointly achieve a task. In organizations it is generally impossible to specify the totality of activities necessary to carry out a task, and much has to be left to the individual's discretion and judgement about his own task, and his relation to others. At this point the social group becomes an important influence in the decision-making process concerning work.

There are a number of ways in which groups can be classified. One of the most frequently discussed distinctions is between formal and informal groups in the organization.

TYPES OF GROUP

> The social organization of the industrial plant is in part formally organized. It is composed of a number of strata or levels ... these levels are well defined and all the formal orders, instructions and compensations are addressed to them. And such functions taken together make up the formal organization of the plant. It includes the systems, policies, rules and regulations of the plant which expresses what the relations of one person to another are supposed to be in order to achieve effectively the task of technical production. It prescribes the relations that are supposed to obtain within the human organization. In short, the pattern of human inter-relations as defined by the systems, rules, policies and regulations of the company constitute the formal organiz-ation. (Roethlisberger and Dickson[1].)

Formal Groups

These patterns of human interrelations manifest themselves at the interpersonal level, in formal group and role relations.

Formal groups are created to achieve specific objectives which are deliberately and, hopefully, clearly related to the organization's goals. Most formal groups are of a permanent nature, even though their membership may change from time to time as employees leave and new members replace them. However, organizations create temporary formal groups to deal with specific problems— project teams for example, or personnel policy committees. In formal groups the task predominates. It brings people together whose cohesion rests upon the successful meshing of *role* relationships—work activities. Frequently, the formal work group has no choice over a new member, especially at the lower levels of an industrial hierarchy. Since the roles may be well defined, in job descriptions or by the technology, the source of group cohesion can, initially at least for a new member or new work group, rest on formal role relationships. It often happens that only a few informal relationships develop among the members of a group, because the closeness of role specification eliminates need for elaborating the work role, and the technology prevents proximity and shared on-the-job leisure time.

Although the 'team' may be operating co-operatively, such interdependence is ensured by the technology rather than the mutually agreed co-operation of the work 'team'. Other formal groups, however, may dispense with their formal role definition and relationships, replacing these with superior methods of mutual co-operation. These situations may be found in administrative offices, shop-floor work groups and management groups. Changes made with formal organizations in this way are likely to be in the direction of ensuring higher social reward, increased safety from authority, and interpersonal satisfactions of the members.

Informal Groups

All the experimental studies pointed to the fact that there is something more to the social organization than what has been formally recognized. Many of the actually existing patterns of human interaction have no representation in the formal organization at all, and others are adequately represented by the formal organization. (Roethlisberger and Dickson[1].)

In organizations there is both the informal *elaborations of roles* in the formal work group, and the *development of totally informal voluntary groups*. Although the structural influences of work may facilitate or prevent the formation of informal groups in organizations, informal groups rest predominantly on *personal*, rather than *role* relationships. Location, similar status, age, and work roles

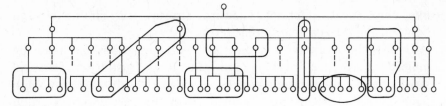

Fig. 5.1 *Informal relationships in a formal organization*

provide the basis on which people may meet and develop personal informal relationships which serve to satisfy needs not directly associated with task achievement, those of friendship, support, a sense of identity, self-esteem.

Argyris[2] noted that industrial organizations often fail to satisfy the affiliative and other social motivations of their members. Where this is so, groups and individuals are likely to devise ways of satisfying these motivations. Informal groups can develop in a variety of directions in the organization. A number of these directional possibilities are illustrated in Fig. 5.1, and they suggest some hypothetical informal groupings of horizontal, vertical, and diagonal cliques. Some informal groupings may coincide with the formal task group, while others elaborate the formal systems, and provide links with parts of formal task groups.

Organizations have a formal system of roles, rules and procedures, observed by individuals and groups. Much elaboration and interpretation of the roles, rules and procedures take place at the informal level, generally receiving the informal but explicit sanction of the working group. The effect of a work-to-rule in an organization shows the importance of such informal interpretations and additions to the rules of conduct governing the enterprise. Indeed the effective operation of an organization depends on a well established informal network of communication, and a body of 'unofficial' norms. Horizontal, vertical and mixed informal cliques of employees at all levels may serve a key communication function, up, down and sideways. When informal communications and other informal practices are in the direction of organizational efficiency, such informal groups are usually vital in maintaining efficiency and morale. When such informal groups and arrangements are contrary to the safe and efficient operation of the organization, then reasons must be sought to explain why informal groups have developed dysfunctional (from the organization point of view) practices. It may well be that relationships outside the organization are an important basis for the formation of such cliques. Generally speaking, however, the formal organization of the work, roles and statuses will be found to be preventing certain inter-personal satisfactions, creating stresses and strains in and between individuals at different levels.

Under the formal structure of work, relationships may be inhibiting effective working and generating frustration. Personal satisfactions have subsequently been sought in informal groupings. Such informal groups may coincide with the task group (a group of interdependent operatives), or be formed from groups of similar level employees, drawn from larger, separate groups (for example, a group of departmental maintenance engineers who develop a code of informal working to rule). The emergence of informal groups and relationships within the organization may also occur as a result of the inappropriateness of the formal arrangements and the difficulties of working according to the formal rules and procedures. Informal groupings may also develop in response to perceived threats and insecurity, e.g. they can develop as a form of protection from authority, in response to change programmes, which because they are implemented with little references to those who will be affected by the changes, stimulate informal working arrangements among organization members.

DIFFERENTIATING BETWEEN FORMAL AND INFORMAL GROUPS

The examination of the informal groups and their relationships within an organization is often one of the early steps taken by behavioural scientists when researching into an organization to find out its most appropriate structure, or to explore why reporting relationships and communications are confused. Among methods used to determine the informal groupings and structure is one which requires the organization's members to nominate their superiors, peers and subordinates, and also to nominate individuals with whom they have frequent contact. A typical way of establishing the informal working relationship would be to ask:

Who are you most dependent on to do your job well?
Who is dependent on you to do their job well?
Who are you responsible for?
Who is responsible for you?

The relationships and groupings which members report can then be compared with the formal organization chart as top management perceive it.

An example of a result obtained from such an enquiry is given below. The formal organization structure is given in Fig. 5.2 and the relationships which actually existed, in Fig. 5.3.

From Fig. 5.3 it can be seen that a group has formed itself

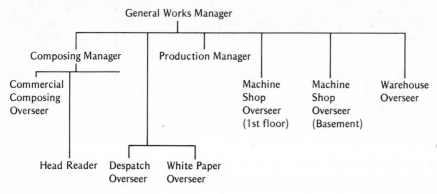

Fig. 5.2 *The formal system*

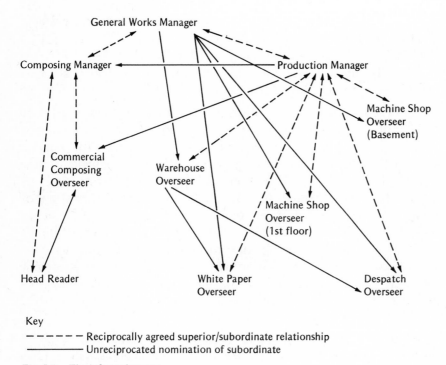

Key

– – – – – Reciprocally agreed superior/subordinate relationship
——————— Unreciprocated nomination of subordinate

Fig. 5.3 *The informal system*

around the Production Manager, which in part effectively isolates the General Works Manager. However, the informal grouping reflects the requirements of day to day working arrangements, and while this informal structure may not be wholly appropriate, in itself it is a partial consequence of the inadequacies of the formal organization structure.

How far should a manager go in formalizing informal work arrangements? The organization as a unit conventionally tends towards formalizing relationships. The need for measures and predictors of performance, policies, standards, procedures, and rules, press the manager into rationalizing and formalizing the arrangements and activities of groups. This may certainly be necessary. However, Sadler and Barry[3] suggest that the following process of analysis should be carried out in examining the various contributions of informal activities:

(1) Examine the work flow to see what relationships are needed.
(2) Decide where the formal organization meets these requirements and where it does not.
(3) Find out what informal methods of coping exist.
(4) Find out what formal channels do exist to facilitate relationships outside the chain of command, and evaluate their effectiveness.
(5) Decide which informal methods to formalize.
(6) Decide (devise) ways of facilitating those which are best left to operate informally.

In motivational terms, informal work arrangements provide important sources of satisfaction for an organization's members. Among these will be the satisfactions associated with making decisions about, and controlling, work activities. Individuals may develop an 'emotional' investment in the informal work arrangements they have helped to construct, and the formalization of them by management may reduce the personal incentives to maintain an activity that could be important to the organization's functioning. In considering the formalization of informal procedures and the rationalization of informal groups, management must take special account of the motivational consequences for members of informal structures.

LARGE AND SMALL GROUPS

It is helpful to refer to *large* (secondary) groups and to *small* (primary) groups, and to polarize their main characteristics. Like most classifications, however, groups will, in reality, be seen to have certain aspects of both the types.

SECONDARY GROUPS (large) *are relatively*	PRIMARY GROUPS (small) *are relatively*
impersonal,	intimate,
formal,	informal,
instrumental,	affective,
role relationship predominant.	personal, rather than role relationship predominant.

Normally, small primary groups (work groups) develop within the boundaries of large secondary groups (departments). However, primary groups often emerge linking members of different larger groups, for example, an informal group of departmental secretaries who meet regularly, or foremen of several different production departments, or representatives of a Union.

The size of a group influences its behaviour. At about twelve members a group will usually begin to split into smaller units. Research by Seashore[4] suggests that group cohesiveness (defined as the attractiveness of the group to the members) is inversely correlated with size—that is, the smaller the group the greater the cohesion. Beyond a certain size, problems of communications and those of emotional satisfactions mentioned above, cause individuals (environment and situation permitting) to seek smaller groupings.

All groups carry out transactions across their boundaries. New members are taken in and others excluded, and information and materials are exchanged. The management of these exchanges, the boundary regulations of the group, is one of the functions of group leadership which may be vested in one person, or shared by several.

> The extent to which transactions across the boundary display consistency is one measure of the extent to which the members are emotionally committed to their group. Miller and Rice[5]

Emotional commitment to a group implies the development of personal relationships as well as role relationships, that is, relationships between members of a group are not determined solely by roles, formally given, but become overlaid with values and feelings shared personally, and expressed in varying degrees emotionally. It is therefore a little misleading to refer to formal and informal groupings as such—most groups combine elements of formal role relationships with informal personal relationships.

Large groups are normally internally differentiated. If they are not, it is likely that they will be relatively short lived. Miller and Rice point out that they are 'correspondingly more prone to be dominated by irrational assumptions'. Thus rumour may abound and individuals lose their sense of identity. Behaviour may be individually unobservable, anonymity prevails and social pressure (informal sanctions) are ignored, put aside and simply do not develop.

Formal, informal, small, large: these and other characteristics of many work groups are in part determined by the structure of *Tasks* (the layout of the plant and work flow)—in part by the

GROUPS AND
THEIR TASKS

technology. This is naturally most influential at the level of those actually operating the technology.

Technology and work layouts determine the nature of large groups. Production lines, for example, usually require more people than a small face-to-face group could accommodate. Furthermore, the nature of the work may effectively prevent a large group from differentiating itself internally into a number of smaller working groups. In such situations one may expect that the control of employees' behaviour will be a function mainly of the technology, supervisory activities, and the internalized standards of the employee. One of the major functions of the smaller group is that it can provide for the individual personal relationships, and certain inter-personal satisfactions. Because membership can be denied by other members, work behaviour can, in part, be controlled by the personal relationships which develop out of work relationships. Important local controls over behaviour can be exerted in this way—albeit, not always in the best interests of production and efficiency. Small groups provide the member with a test of perceptual reality, i.e., he can test what he feels and sees against others, using the group as a yardstick. In the absence of small groupings, uncertainty may develop. Further, the large undifferentiated group may act out leadership (power) problems, with open hostility towards the 'others' (probably management), in the same way that football crowds and other large and undifferentiated groups can manifest 'irrational' behaviour.

It has been frequently observed that low morale (expressed in 'low' attitude towards management and the job) is associated with large concentrations of employees doing similar tasks. Aspects of technology which are associated with such large concentrations of employees will undoubtedly be those of simple, routine, repetitive work, and this in itself is a further contribution to low morale, by the denial of intrinsic work satisfactions. Where work is simplified, repetitive, and routine, large groups will consist of a relative homogeneous membership. Sayles[6] has noted that size and homogeneity of membership combine with potent effect.

> What seems essential for verbalizing complaints and uniting people to 'fight them', was some reinforcement ... provided by people having identical experiences where each one could hear his own grievance repeated and magnified ... with sympathetic repetition the problem grew in importance.

Homogeneity contributes to concerted group action, and in large undifferentiated group behaviour, such group action is more likely to develop on 'irrational assumptions'.

In Sayles's studies an especially significant finding was the 'striking similarity in technological characteristics among groups that behave similarly'. At the most general level group behaviour in the plant can be explained as the groups' inherent ability to function in a certain way, e.g., technology and organization constrain the group to a limited, and hence possibly predictable range of behaviour. Technology sharpens the relationships both between the groups (for example, between different work groups and between management and work groups) and within the groups. Sayles classified work group grievance behaviour into four characteristic forms: apathetic, erratic, strategic, and conservative, all clearly linked with distinctive technological characteristics of the task.

The degree of grievance behaviour, (e.g., work groups/management relationships) whether of a passive or active kind, Sayles shows, is influenced by the following variables.

(1) Relative position of the group on the promotional 'ladders' of the plant.
(2) Relative size and importance of the group.
(3) Similarity of jobs within the group.
(4) The degree to which the work is indispensable in the functioning of the plant or department.
(5) The precision with which management can measure work load and pace for the group.

These variables are largely technologically determined, but it is also the case that relationships between groups are partly influenced by the *internal* structure of the work groups—and this in turn is also related to the technology of the production. The design of the plant will effect the degree of differentiation of the task. The more differentiated the task, the more complicated the social structure and the less grievance reinforcement there is likely to be. Frequency of interaction of group members and the process of leadership will also, in large part, be determined by the technology and work flow.

While technology is shown by Sayles and others to determine in large part patterns of interaction between and within work groups, this does not mean that it is not possible to do anything about ineffective and troublesome work groups. Work flow systems create role relationships between people. The demands of the work flow can generate status differentials, place individuals into potentially antagonistic relationships with each other, and structure pay differences. The work flow can therefore interfere with the successful meshing of role and consequently personal relationships.

Part of the solution to these problems lies in perceiving role and personal relationships within groups as part of the total work system which consists of both a *technical* and a *social* sub-system (i.e., the *socio-technical system*—see chapter 6). Attention must be directed to the design of the technical and social parts of the system in order to build in the possibility of other than economic rewards to accrue to the group members.

Achievement of social and other work related rewards, e.g., job satisfaction, responsibility, sharing, will require the design of a work flow system which allows for role relationships not inimical to these social and psychological rewards. Small group experiments show that co-operative attitudes are brought about by an inter-dependent division of labour, and incentives based on group performance. One of the best examples of the effects of two different social systems on production and attitudes in identical technologies is described in the research carried out by the Tavistock Institute of Human Relations in the Durham coalfield.*

The pre-mechanization, or *traditional single place*, coal mining technology was based on a simple small group organization. Work was done with hand tools, and performance depended on an intimate knowledge of the mine. Members of a group were self-selected, and were multi-skilled all-round workers performing, as a joint undertaking, the entire cycle of extracting coal. The group performed without supervision, in dispersed self-contained locations. It was paid as a group, and developed high adaptability to local working conditions. Management was represented in the work area by an official who performed various services including safety, inspection and setting wage incentive payments. This management system was effective because each work group had developed responsible autonomy, and because the entire production system was slow, requiring little co-ordination at the coal face.

The successor to the single place system was a partially and unevenly mechanized technology. This new organization, known as the *conventional longwall* system, reflected in its design and work roles the prevailing outlook of mass production engineering.

Mine output depended on completion of the working cycle, which consisted of 'preparing' an area for coal extraction, 'getting' and removing coal with the aid of conveyors and 'advancing' the machinery and roadways. This whole cycle was carried out over three shifts. On each eight-hour shift one or more task groups

* The authors would like to thank Dr Hugh Murray of the Tavistock Institute for permission to reproduce in large part his account of the coalmining study.(7)

performed their work, provided that the preceding tasks had been completed. The coal removal tasks were the most onerous, and non-completion frequently impeded the work cycle, reducing output. Having been assigned a specialized task and an ostensibly equal work load, each worker was paid an incentive to perform his task without reference to the other tasks of co-workers in his, or other, task groups.

The consequence of this was the development of isolated task groups, each with its own customs, agreements with management, and payment arrangements related to its own interests. Co-ordination between men and groups on different shifts, and control of work, had to be provided entirely from outside, by management. To be effective, control had to be coercive, which was both unsuitable and impracticable in the high-risk coal face environment. Management lacked the means to weld the individual task groups into an integrated team for performance of the cycle as a whole, and inter-group co-ordination could not develop. The inability to develop work-team relationships resulted in hostility and conflict among groups of workers, and between them and management. Each worker and task group viewed the assigned task in isolation.

When mine conditions were bad, or prior work was not completed, the individual could not cope and would wait for management to take corrective action, or indeed he would just not turn up for work. The lowest level of management in the mine spent most of its time in emergency action over technical breakdowns, system dysfunctioning, and bargaining with workers over special payment to have the resulting abnormal tasks completed.

In the alternative system known as the *composite longwall* system, a group of 41 miners were associated with the whole 24 hour task by:

(a) a common paynote reflecting output over the 24 hours;
(b) task versatility as distinct from task specialization;
(c) shift rotation, enabling social relationships to be built up within the group responsible for the whole task.

Self-selected groups of 41 men allocated themselves to jobs and shifts over the whole 24 hour cycle and received payment on the basis of the overall level of output achieved. Work flow arrangements had been amended, with an appropriate redesign of the social system, so as to permit superior meshing of role-relationships and interdependence between the shift groups.

Setting goals for the performance of the entire cycle, and making inclusive payments to the group as a whole for the completion of all the tasks in the cycle, plus an incentive for output, placed responsibility on the entire group for all operations, generating the need for individuals performing different tasks over interdependent phases of the cycle to interrelate. The establishment of equal earnings led to the spontaneous development of interchangeability of workers according to need. Interchangeability required development of multi-skilled face workers and permitted sharing the common fund of skill and experience.

The method of work employed in each shift was directed at maintaining task continuity. Each shift picked up where the previous shift left off, and when a particular group's main task was done, it redeployed itself to carry on with the next task even if this meant starting a new cycle. All of the required roles were internally allocated to members by the work group as it developed responsible autonomous behaviour. Equalized opportunity for good and bad work-times was thus afforded. Teams as a whole also worked out their own system for rotating tasks and shift. Each team was of sufficient size to make enough men available to fill the roles that arose on each shift.

The autonomous cycle group thus integrated the differentiated activities of longwall mining, by internal self-managing mechanisms. By contrast the integration practices used in conventional longwall mining were those of indirect external control, through specialization of tasks with fixed assignments, wage incentive bargaining for each task and skimpy attempts at direct supervision.

The significance of the alternative composite method of self-managing work groups is contained in the data for conventional and composite working. The composite form of organization provided a greater and richer variety of work experience. In teams of 41 men, on average a man worked at only one main task under conventional organization as against $3\frac{1}{2}$ main tasks on composite faces; a man worked in only one activity group on conventional, whereas on composite on average the experience was in $5\frac{1}{2}$ different activity groups. Where changing or sharing of stressful tasks was not possible, it contributed to withdrawal or absence from work. If a man is 'tied' to his work place under stressful conditions, there is an increased likelihood that accidents may occur; he may become sick or simply not turn up for work. The overall absence rates were 20 per cent on the conventional compared with 8 per cent on the composite. The comparable rate for the percentage of manshifts lost arising from accidents were 7 per cent and 3 per cent respectively; from sickness 9 per cent and $4\frac{1}{2}$ per cent, and voluntary absence 4 per cent and $2\frac{1}{2}$ per cent. This last figure gives a good indication of the extent to which the composite face team was committed to the success of its enterprise.

It may be inferred that absence rates had an effect on the state of cycle progress—the extent to which the operational system was under control. At the end of the shift on which coal is conveyed from the face, the cycle state was lagging on the conventional face on 69 per cent of cycles, compared with 5 per cent on the composite; the cycle state was never in advance of the shift on the conventional production system, while it was in advance 22 per cent of the time under the composite organization. So usual was cycle lag on the conventional that it required an average manpower reinforcement of 6 per cent per week. When lag did occur on the composite face, counteraction was taken by the work group itself, mainly through the practice of task continuity, so it maintained itself without manpower reinforcement. As for regularity of production, the conventional, with conditions quite normal, ran for only 12 weeks before 'losing a cycle'. On the other hand, the composite ran for 65 weeks. As regards level of productivity, the conventional achieved 78 per cent of the face potential and the composite 95 per cent.

It is obvious that the mining team with the composite organization was a highly motivated and commited group. The example demonstrates the necessity of designing production systems which create the conditions under which such commitment can develop. In the discussion of motivation (chapter 4), some main psychological requirements which people have from work were outlined. Many of these requirements: variety, decision-making (a degree of autonomy), social support, etc., can be met, in part, from the individuals' interdependence with others in the working group. A group will have its strongest motivational effect when its members (and this includes all levels of employees) are primarily related to each other as a result of the requirements of task performance and task interdependence.

Miller and Rice[5] note some of the main requirements of autonomous work groups. These requirements point to the necessity of designing groups and tasks jointly to produce an optimum solution to the problems which arise as a result of social needs of employees and the technical-economic needs of production. They are:

- The task must be such that those engaged with parts can experience, as a group, the completion of the 'whole' task.
- The group must be able to regulate its own activities and be judged by results. (That is, in system terms, a group should be able to control the input/output processes of the group.*)

(* Author's additions.)

- The group has to be of such a size that it cannot only regulate its own activities, but also provides satisfactory personal relationships. (This seems to be a highly variable figure. Groups of eight have been said to be an optimum size, but in the mining example the total group size was 41.*)
- The range of skills required in the group for task performance must not be as great as to reinforce external affiliations and thus induce internal differentiation. Nor should status difference in the group be large enough to inhibit internal mobility.

In the development of autonomous work groups, the role relationships within the groups can often become overlaid with emotional interdependence. At this point the task group becomes identical with the 'emotional' group—called the *sentient* group. Miller and Rice[5] say:

The task/sentient group should not be unique, so that those who become disaffected have no alternative group engaged on a similar task and requiring similar skills and experience to which they can move. Otherwise the investment in the group is likely to be so great as to distort values and judgements, and the possibility of expulsion so threatening as to be destructive.

Such a level of commitment to any group has obvious implications for a group's internal structure and change, and its relationships with other groups.

Indeed, more recent studies have shown that groups where *task* and *human* needs are optimized, and where there are satisfying social relationships, may be highly resistant to change. The problems encountered with the introduction of the conventional longwall system of mining were partly a consequence of lack of appreciation that in the traditional work group task and sentient group boundaries coincided. This may point to new complexities underlying the successful design of *tasks, work groups,* and other social groupings, as many different aspects of work situations will require integrated planning and design. Above all, it points to the special significance of informal groups for certain types of work satisfactions.

A WIDER VIEW
An understanding of behaviour in groups cannot be obtained solely from reference to the internal workings of the group. Individuals are members of many groups. In fact groups are the micro-societies

in which people spend their lives. People possess multiple roles: father, son, neighbour, manager, colleague, subordinate, etc., some of which are acted out in relatively durable groups (the family, the work group) and others of which, like the role of juror, course member, are held for shorter periods in temporary groups. Groups, in the sense that roles are played in them, act as a major influence controlling behaviour. They exert pressure upon members to ensure a degree of conformity to standards. Such pressure, from multiple group membership, ensures, along with an internalized need to behave according to learned standards, the general control of behaviour. The pressure that a group exerts upon its members rests in the final analysis upon the ability to reject or exclude a member.

Continuous conflict between the demands of various groups usually is avoidable because the roles which people have in them are temporally and spatially separated. Group standards, however, often do have a powerful influence over behaviour, even when a person is in a different group from the one whose standards are influencing him. Such ambivalence about, and conflict between, standards causes stress and anxiety for the individual. Conflicts of this kind exist at some time for most people, and as a result behaviour is continually being adjusted in various group settings to accommodate the requirements of one group against those of another. An alternative way of looking at this is to realize that many apparently disparate groups are linked through one individual, each group at separate or similar times making its demand upon that individual. Some groups are interconnected with common elements of membership and shared values. But work and family may conflict in their demands, as may a business role, and in a strict interpretation of Christian values. However, a specially important aspect of group membership is that the selection of groups to which individuals belong, and the rejection of others, reflects a desire to belong to the social groupings in which personally held values and beliefs receive support.

Thus, understanding behaviour requires consideration of group demands on an individual if an adequate explanation is to be found. Signs of neurosis, anxiety, ineffectiveness and non-cooperation may be indications of the incompatible demands of the roles an individual holds in a number of other groups, and the problems that this causes for effective social interaction.

In advanced urban industrial societies people have many temporary and relatively anonymous activities for day-to-day living, as a customer, for instance, or a passenger, which do not take place within a group context. In such situations behaviour is governed by internalized standards and a knowledge of the various role expectations which are generalized in society. In small primitive communities, such anonymous relationships may be unnecessary and inconceivable since all relationships are mediated through ascribed roles and statuses in a number of key groups: family, tribe, territorial group. Anonymous instrumental relationships abound in Western society, and this has placed special importance on a small number of significant primary groups (the family, the peer and the working group) to provide a number of emotional needs.

Furthermore, modern society is partly characterized by the temporariness of many of the groups to which people have to belong, and particularly this is so for the work group. Our fractionated and mobile society brings all manner of people into formal groups for the purpose of work, and it is not surprising therefore that groups often face problems of cohesion, stability, teamwork and communication. The highly specialized character of individual skills and knowledge, the temporariness of groups, the pressure to improve one's effectiveness and use of time, and differing emotional and personal needs, can all present difficulties for the formation and maintenance of effective work groups, especially in management.

> Management will make full use of the potential capabilities of its human resources only when each person in an organization is a member of one or more effectively functioning work groups that have a high degree of loyalty, effective skills of interaction and high performance goals (Rensis Likert[8]).

There is a growing interest in the functioning of management groups and in the need to build effective teams of individuals. Organizations depend on the effectiveness of cooperation, communication, creativity, and the problem-solving activity of their work groups—and most especially of their managerial work groups. There has therefore been increasing interest shown in the development in managers of those social interaction skills which help to ensure group effectiveness. This process of changing or developing managers' social interaction skills, such as group management or leadership, in line with an overall shift in organizational values and climate, is called *Organizational Development* (See chapter 11). A large part of organizational development is aimed at the improved effectiveness of inter- and intra-group working. Likert's concepts of interlocking groups, and supportive relationships within groups are an example of such an approach. Warren Bennis's model of 'planned change'[9] involves the collaborative changing of values

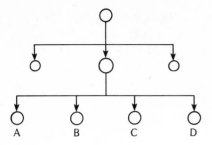

Fig. 5.4 *Managing the individual*

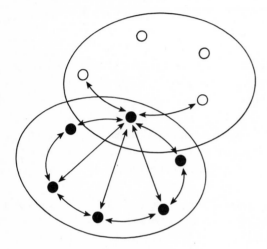

Fig. 5.5 *Managing relationships*

and activities in the enterprise such that among other things there is the generation of increased understanding between and within working groups, and the development of more effective team management.

The concept of the autonomous working group, therefore, has its managerial equivalent in the 'project' team, or 'group' management; where the intention is to enhance and develop:

    (a) relationships within and between groups,
    (b) mutual confidence and trust,
    (c) interdependence and shared responsibility,
    (d) multi-group membership and responsibility,
    (e) wide sharing of control and responsibility,
    (f) conflict resolution through bargaining and problem solving.

A simple example of the form of change envisaged is illustrated in Figs. 5.4 and 5.5. In Fig. 5.4 the manager typically manages his subordinates as individuals on the principle of a one-to-one relationship. The group is basically regarded as a number of relatively separate individuals, and interdependence between them, and collective autonomy, is undeveloped.

While communication may take place between A, B, C and D, there is little shared responsibility, and conflict is resolved by the decision of the manager. In this arrangement the responsibility for the task of the unit is perceived as 'belonging' to the manager above, while A, B, C, and D have responsibility for their subordinates' collective task. Management groups are as much a socio-technical system as are manufacturing groups (with the technical element represented by formal rules, procedures, and work flow). The ideal socio-technical system is one in which the technical aspect of work is organized in such a manner that the immediate work group has a meaningful unit of activity, some degree of responsibility for its task and a satisfactory set of interpersonal relationships.

An alternative approach (Fig. 5.5) which requires changes in the work flow system, recognizes that a manager in an organization is a member of one formal group in the organization with his superior, and a leader in his own group. He therefore serves as a 'linking pin' between the two groups.

Recognition of this 'boundary' management position implies increased autonomy for those who are a manager's subordinates. Such autonomy may be most appropriate in the context of a team which develops the characteristics described above.

As has already been seen from the coal mining study, participation in decision-making tends to create a higher level of commitment to the task, and democratic discussion facilitates communication and cohesion in the group. It also brings the group pressure of a collective decision to bear on task performance. It generates helping relationships in which the specific ideas and talents of individuals may become known and used by the group.

New forms of organized structure are developing within the confines of the traditional organization model. More radical departures will, in all likelihood, arise in firms whose environment and technology require especially adaptive systems. Relationships between individuals will probably be increasingly governed by membership of 'problem-centred', probably multi-disciplinary teams, rather than membership of a status level in a functionally specialized segment of the organization, with one boss and intermittent relationships with a host of other specialized segments. Multi-group membership will be more common, with problems of getting on with a wide range of different disciplines and hence people with potentially different perceptions of business objectives.

Coupled with social, economic and technical changes, the implications for management skills are plain. If human and group relations skills were appropriate to the management of traditional hierarchical organizations, their necessity under new conditions is much more evident.

REFERENCES

(1) Roethlisberger, F. J., and Dickson, W. J., *Management and the Worker,* Harvard University Press, 1939.
(2) Argyris, C. *Integrating the Individual and the Organization,* New York: Wiley, 1964.
(3) Sadler, P. J., and Barry, B. A., *Organizational Development: Case Studies in the Printing Industry,* Longmans, 1970.
(4) Seashore, S. E., *Group Cohesiveness in the Industrial Work Group,* University of Michigan, 1954.
(5) Miller, E. J. and Rice, A. K., *Systems of Organization: Task and Sentient Systems and their Boundary Control,* Tavistock Publications, 1967.
(6) Sayles, L. R., *Behaviour of Industrial Work Groups,* New York: Wiley, 1958.
(7) Murray, H., 'An introduction to socio-technical systems at the level of the primary work group,' *Tavistock Institute of Human Relations Doc.* No. HRC 492, 1970.
(8) Likert, R. L., *The Human Organization: its Management and Value,* New York: McGraw Hill, 1967.
(9) Bennis, W. G., *Changing Organizations,* New York: McGraw Hill, 1966.

6
Organizations as systems

An organization can be viewed in terms of its:

> *Task*, e.g., specific goals in relation to the environment;
> *Technology*, e.g., equipment and process;
> *Structure*, e.g., size, internal differentiation, formal relation-ships;
> *People*, e.g., the skill, knowledge, personality characteristics and motivations of personnel.

These 'elements' are highly interdependent; changes in any one of them will bring about changes in varying degrees in the others. The characteristics of any one of these elements will have an effect in determining the characteristics of the others. The task of an organization and the constraints placed upon it by the environment will help to determine the kinds of equipment and processes used. The technology will require certain types and levels of mental and physical abilities, will shape groupings of people and their relationships. The method of manufacturing will induce structural characteristics in the organization, for example in large buying departments and stores, work study, and methods engineering departments. Historically, attempts to improve organizations have tended to focus predominantly on only one of the above elements with little recognition of its interdependence with the others, and consequently often with harmful effects.

There are two schools of management theory which need introduction before approaching a contemporary perspective of organizations. The *classical management theory* school evolved a number of principles of organization which were thought to be applicable to all organizations. Their prescriptions were chiefly *structural*, that is, concerned with the anatomy of the organization. This school stated that there is a limit to the number of subordinates a man can control (generally put at about eight to ten); that each man should have one boss and one boss only; that the executive should delegate both responsibility and authority to subordinates but cannot relinquish responsibility; that there should be organization-wide rules and procedures governing members' behaviour; that authority is derived from the office.

Important considerations though these may be, social research and experience demonstrate their limitations. The other variables in the enterprise, the characteristics of the *people*, the nature of the *task*, and the *technology*, influence the applicability of these prescriptions. Spans of control are known to vary (but be successfully managed) from one to thirty in management groups. Some organizations have members who have a number of bosses rather than one boss. Responsibility has sometimes to be relinquished where there is a wide difference in the expertise of 'boss' and 'subordinate'; delegative responsibility means making people *accountable* for their actions. Organization-wide rules may interfere with the freedom of specialized and different functions to do their particular task in the appropriate manner. Furthermore, in specialized and highly skilled activities, authority evidently does rest more on individual characteristics such as ability, knowledge, reputation, rather than rest on the 'office' and its attendant official status.

The second approach to organizations reflects a different philosophy about control and authority, and is known as the *Human Relations School of Management*. The development of this approach was in a large measure derived from the experience of the Hawthorne studies described in chapter 4. Its focus is on raising human performance in the enterprise by improving the human relations' climate and the social rewards experienced by employees. Specifically this school has been associated with calls for participative management, human relations and leadership training, group working and wider employee control in the work place.

Such prescriptions indicate important strategies for improving organizations, though often they are used to handle stresses which may arise out of structural inadequacies. Again, what is an appropriate provision in terms of a social and psychological reward from work, is dependent in part on the interacting requirments of the task, technology and structure. The task of crisis management, with fail-dangerous technology, give rise to certain types of structures (hierarchy, high degree of specialization and close supervision of work, among other things), which limits the extent to which human relations prescriptions are applicable.

These two schools of organization and management theory imply a generally applicable organizational form. The reality of organization, however, is that they should be unique and purpose-built out of the demands of their particular circumstances.

Today, it is usual to conceive of organizations as systems with the above variables in a complex interdependence, each in part determining the other's characteristics. It is important to realize that there is no one good organization, but only organizations which are more or less well fitted to the demands of the task, the constraints of the technology, and the needs of the organization rather than any single element in it.

The four variables in organization interact to shape the character of three major processes in the enterprise. Recent work identified three major organizational processes which are necessary for the achievement of the overall task. These are the processes of *control*, *integration*, and *boundary* regulation. Briefly, these processes refer to:

(a) Control—the organization needs to ensure that individuals perform their work activities in a manner which leads to the achievement of the task.

(b) Integration—'whereas control is concerned with the ways in which the activity components of roles are defined and regulated, integration is concerned with the ways in which the relationship component of roles are defined and regulated'[1].

(c) Boundary regulations—the organization must also ensure that the internal behaviour of the enterprise is sufficiently 'open' to the environment in which the organization must survive to ensure the appropriate adaptation of its task, structures, etc.

There is a range of strategies open to management in achieving a solution to these problems. The strategies which are chosen will in part be influenced by the interdependent variables in organization, which have been briefly outlined above, and which can best be comprehended by employing the systems approach to organization.

THE SYSTEMS APPROACH[2]

The systems approach to viewing organizations has been found to be of great value in understanding what happens in them. The concept of a system is of common use in biology with respect to organisms[3]. An organism will take in something from the environment, convert it, and export something back into the environment. In so doing the organism itself will change. The human being for example imports into itself food, water, air, and information, converts these in terms of the needs of its own mental and organic functioning, and exports back into the environment activities and waste products.

This notion of input-conversion-output can readily be applied to organizations in that they take in resources (people, raw materials, energy, etc.) from the environment, convert them, and return them to the environment in various forms. An organization will be viable provided its output to the environment meets an environmental need greater than the cost of its inputs and conversion process, and in the case of a profit organization, the revenue from its output is consistent. As the environment is comprised of other systems, one system's (or organization's) output can be regarded as the input for another. If other systems do not want the outputs of the first system, then the viability of the first system is threatened; it can either die (that is, it refuses to change), or it can alter its outputs so that they become those which are needed. When altering its outputs the system will usually change its conversion process and its inputs. Therefore, if the environment consists of many systems all importing, converting and exporting, then all these systems are in varying degrees of strength dependent upon each other (that is, a system which changes its input requirements will cast around until it finds these new requirements, and these new requirements will come from other systems having to change their outputs).

An organization should be sufficiently aware, or open, to detect that its output is not relevant to the needs of other organizations; when it has done this, it should then have the capability of changing or adapting its output so that it does become needed. An organization can go one step further in that it can identify potential needs of other systems, and do something in advance about meeting those needs. Organizations which are capable of appropriately adapting to changing needs are frequently described as open systems.

OPEN AND CLOSED SYSTEMS

Figure 6.1 illustrates the conversion process with the necessary feedbacks of information to ensure adaptation and change. It is important to note that feedback is always available, but whether the organization either chooses to, or is capable of, acting on it, is another matter.

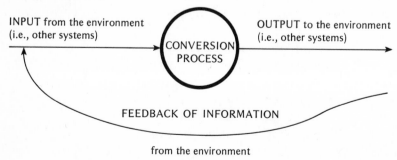

INPUT from the environment (i.e., other systems)

CONVERSION PROCESS

OUTPUT to the environment (i.e., other systems)

FEEDBACK OF INFORMATION

from the environment

Fig. 6.1   *The organization as a conversion process*

Usually organizations are highly selective in the feedback they 'hear' and act upon. A technologically dominant company, for example, will tend to be more concerned with the performance of its products than with whether its products are selling profitably or are indeed really necessary.

The outputs and the conversion process frequently determine the inputs of organizations in such a way that the organization gets itself locked into an inward looking self-justifying attitude which has all the characteristics of a system not capable of change, i.e. a closed system.

On the other hand, a few years ago a cigarette lighter manufacturer closely examined and redefined the need which its product was meeting in the market and concluded that it was not really in the cigarette lighter business but in the gift business. In redefining the meaning of the output to the environment, the organization revised its inputs and conversion processes and found itself in the marketing of products which would have been inconceivable with the earlier thinking.

INTERDEPEN-
DENCE

An organization consists of many smaller systems, 'sub' input-conversion-output systems, all of which are in some way inter-dependent, in that one sub-system's output is another's input. This is well illustrated when a sub-system ceases to function. In such a case, the viability of the organization may be threatened, unless it can change this sub-system or 'grow' other sub-systems to compensate. For example, financial accounting has undergone rapid changes in the past decade, yet some financial departments are too 'closed' to acknowledge this. As a result, some organizations find themselves taking critical decisions on the wrong data. Such financial departments are usually very strong and are not easily changed. In consequence, many other sub-systems begin to compensate for the inadequate outputs. Such activities as company planning, or management accounting, while usually legitimately adding to an organization, sometimes arise as 'by-pass' mechanisms for this purpose.

Taking the concept of interdependence within an organization a step further, it follows that changes made within a sub-system of an organization will in some way effect other sub-systems. For example a new procedure (conversion process) within the cost accounting department may mean new inputs from other departments which they are not geared up to give, and also may change the character of the cost accounting department's output which other sub-systems may not be in a position to use. The

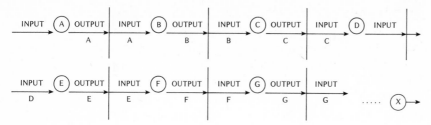

Fig. 6.2 *Organizations as a set of sub-systems*

introduction of a computer into an organization is another example. There are many instances of the difficulties experienced in doing this, but many of these difficulties could have been at least predicted (and hence action taken) if the highly inter-dependent nature of the organization had been appreciated.

Manifestations of interdependence of course go beyond immedi-ately related departments. A mismatch between one system's output and another's input is likely to be a source of trouble, the symptom of which may appear at some distance from the actual cause. Given the sequential nature in the arrangement of the sub-systems in a typical organization, it is possible to trace the cause of a presenting problem back to a mismatch of an output and input which may be located at a considerable 'distance' from the apparent difficulty.

In Fig. 6.2 if an error occurs in output A, and is not detected by sub-system A, then it can manifest itself at any point down the line. If the presenting symptom occurs at G for example, the people operating that sub-system are most likely (but not always) to blame F. The result is that tension will arise between G and F, which in itself could become disruptive, whilst A proceeds happily and innocently along.

To cope with such potentially disruptive variations in the quality of the flow of 'material' between sub-systems, many organizations set up further systems, which are super-ordinate to the production sub-systems, which act as control functions. This is an obvious solution, but it is treating a symptom not a cause. Frequently the most effective control can be built in at the production sub-system level.

A further way of looking at systems is to look into the conversion process itself. All organizations are concerned with the manipu-lation of resources of one kind or another. For ease of remembering, these resources are often called the four Ms—Men, Materials, Machines and Money. At a broader level of explanation

SOCIO-
TECHNICAL
SYSTEMS

an organization's resources divide into two groups—human and non-human. This is a very important distinction because the needs and demands of the human part of the enterprise vary a great deal from the needs and demands of the non-human part. An assembly line should be kept going at a constant speed for 24 hours a day, with breaks only for maintenance, if the investment in the plant and machinery is to be maximized. However, the people who work on the line are much more suited for working for about eight hours a day, with rest pauses, meal breaks and with a working pace which will vary, and which they may wish to control themselves. The requirements of the human and non-human resources, then, differ a great deal, and to meet fully the demands of one without reference to the needs of the other is not the most effective thing to do. Common practice is to meet the non-human demands first, with the result that the people (especially in the assembly line example) tend to be asked to behave like machines, which increasingly they are disinclined to do.

The term *socio-technical system* was first used by researchers at the Tavistock Institute of Human Relations in connection with some studies which were then being carried out into coal mining[4]. It was argued that when conversion processes are regarded as socio-technical systems, then the way in which the people (the social system) are matched to tasks (the technical system), will profoundly effect the way in which the needs of both parts of the system are fulfilled. The concept of *joint optimization* was used to explain the need to avoid maximizing on the requirements of either the social or technical sub-systems, and to optimize only on the socio-technical system. This means in some way taking into account some of the requirements of both of the sub-systems. The needs of the technical sub-system are usually easy to define in quantitative terms, but not so the needs of the social sub-system. The needs which people have at work (i.e., social system needs), however, are being understood more and more. (See chapter 4 on the Changing Relationships between Man and Work.)

Regarding organizations as jointly optimized open socio-technical systems focuses more attention on the relationship between the man and his work, and indeed on the group and their work. Ideally organizations should run as a series of discrete sub-systems where the group running one sub-system has complete control over the input, conversion process, and output. Frequently, however, peoples' responsibilities are only partly coincidental with naturally occurring technical sub-systems, and this can lead to problems of an information flow (i.e. output-input) kind.

Figure 6.3 makes a mismatch look obvious, but usually this is

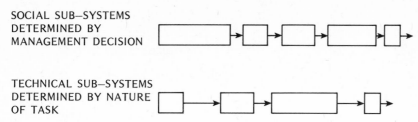

SOCIAL SUB—SYSTEMS
DETERMINED BY
MANAGEMENT DECISION

TECHNICAL SUB—SYSTEMS
DETERMINED BY NATURE
OF TASK

Fig. 6.3 *Mismatch between social and technical sub-systems*

not the case. In order to examine the relationships between the social and technical sub-systems, firstly a thorough understanding of the technical system (or task) is needed. Only by doing this will an appreciation be gained of the naturally occurring sub-systems, i.e., the naturally occurring conversion processes or 'units of operation'[5]. When this has been done the match of people to these units can be looked at. The assumption underlying such an examination is that people should be matched as organizational and social units to the discrete technical sub-systems, or units of operation. Location is of course not enough in itself, because once appropriately located, job content considerations emerge. It may be that because of technological constraints it is impossible to provide tasks which fulfil people's needs from work. The options in this case are to explore automation possibilities, or job enlargement.

The style of managing these now matched social and technical sub-systems can vary. In keeping with what is being found out about motivation it would appear that delegation of authority and responsibility to these units is probably the best thing to do, provided the people operating them have the necessary skills. In these circumstances management can say to a work group that it is responsible for an output of X amount and with a quality range of A to B. The way this is achieved is the responsibility of the group. Management's task then becomes to ensure that this group has all the inputs it needs, and to ensure its output is removed. Included in the input to the group will be feedback on changing needs, and on inappropriate quality or quantity of production, so that it is able to modify its own performance—an uncharacteristic activity of work units where feedback comes from a superordinate control.

Understanding and explaining why certain things happen in organizations, and keeping all these explanations within the framework of one conceptual scheme is highly desirable, indeed vital. The highly complex society in which we live is perhaps best understood in systems terms (witness the current economic-system concerns), which is why this approach is so valuable. As organiz-

73

ation and job design are applied, so will organizations as 'systems' become more and more the perspective employed by management in the design, change and operation of organizations.

REFERENCES

(1) Sadler P. J., and Barry, B. A., *Organizational Development: Case Studies in the Printing Industry,* Longmans, 1970.
(2) Emery, F. E., (ed.) *Systems Thinking,* Penguin, 1969.
(3) von Bertalanffy, L., 'The Theory of Open Systems in Physics and Biology.' In F. Emery (ed.) *Systems Thinking;* Penguin, 1969, pp. 70-85.
(4) Trist, E. L., Higgin, G. W., Murray, H., and Pollock, A. B., *Organizational Choice: Capabilities of Groups at the Coal Face Under Changing Technologies,* Tavistock Publications, 1963.
(5) Herbst, P. G., 'Socio-technical unit design.' *Tavistock Institute of Human Relations Doc.* No. T.899, 1966.

A strategy for understanding organizational problems

It is often difficult to know where to start dealing with organizational problems. A manager may be confronted with considerable complexity, and runs the danger of taking too simple an approach, or dealing with the symptoms rather than the cause.

In chapter 1 a hierarchy of concepts was described to provide a model for ordering and analysing the relationships between component parts of society, and their influence on behaviour. This hierarchy can be reduced to five major sectors:

> the individual
> the role
> the group
> the organization
> the environment

Most problems can be viewed as arising from the relationship, or *interface,* between any two of the above. A person with low job satisfaction for example, can be seen as an example of a mismatch between personal needs (individual) and the demands of the job (role). A company which fails to adapt to changes outside is an example of an organization lacking a function, for example market research, to help it handle the environment. This could be an organization and environment interface problem.

Some problems will be caused by several simultaneous interface difficulties. There may be, for example, both problems between individuals of a personality kind, and problems of a relationship between them and their role kind.

In the process of locating and dealing with interface problems it is useful to follow the scientific procedure of:

diagnosis ———→ prescription ———→ action ———→ evaluation

In this chapter various interfaces are briefly examined by giving typical symptoms, together with an examination of them according to the above steps of diagnosis, prescription, action and evaluation. *It must be emphasized that this is not a comprehensive list, but is intended to indicate a systematic approach to organizational problem solving.* There are fifteen possible interfaces between any two levels in the hierarchy, some of which will occur much more frequently than others when looking at organizational problems.

THE INTERFACES
(a) Individual-Individual

Some Typical Symptoms

Personality clash, 'back-biting', hostility, collusion, lack of co-operation, disputed leadership.

Diagnosis

Incompatibility between two people not related to their organizational roles, or alternatively 'over' compatibility leading to a collusive avoidance of tasks.

Prescription

Take steps to discover source of incompatibility to explore whether it can be altered; similarly the causes for collusion.

Action

Confrontation by a third party of the problem with those involved. This could involve counselling type interviews, and forms of sensitivity training (qv chapter 9). Alternatively, prevent the individuals from having to work together.

Evaluation

Check whether they are able to work effectively together.

(b) Individual-Role

Some Typical Symptoms

Poor job performance, high labour turnover, absenteeism, accidents, lack of co-operation, stress and anxiety in the individual.

Diagnosis

Job is too demanding, job is not demanding enough.

Prescription

Make job less demanding, make job more demanding, i.e. change job. Make man better, replace man, i.e. change man.

Action

Old man in old job, i.e. man retrained 'up' (where do new tasks come from?) Old man in new job, i.e. job redesigned 'down' (where do old tasks go?)

Evaluation

At prescription stage decide on performance criteria.

76

Individual appears to be apart from the group. In cases of the legislated 'leader' of the group, he is isolated and out of touch with the group. A group member actively seeks relationships outside this group.

The individual, by virtue of the sort of person he is, is not acceptable to the group. His 'style' of operating contradicts group values (qv chapter 4 the Hawthorne studies—ratebusting).

Diagnosis

Investigate possibilities of one or both parties changing in order to accommodate. If not possible, remove the individual from the group.

Prescription

A sensitivity training type event to explore the relationship between the group and the individual. This could well include team building.

Action

Check on whether the individual and the group are working together.

Evaluation

(d) Individual-Organization
Some Typical Symptoms

Indifference to job and organizational objectives; working to the 'letter of the law'.

Individuals are not able to relate themselves in a meaningful way to the objectives of the organization and hence withdraw in a variety of ways.

Diagnosis

Explore the difficulty associated with the 'relating'. It may be associated with the unclear nature of the objectives, or clash of organizational objectives and individual values.

Prescription

Attitude survey to find out how individuals perceive the organization. Embark on a programme of relating individual values and company objectives by such methods as 'open' dissemination and debate of a company philosphy/policy document.

Action

Continuous monitoring of the individual/organization relationship.

Evaluation

(e) Individual-Environment
Some Typical Symptoms

General 'withdrawal' from work, e.g., lateness, absenteeism, distraction, apathy, carelessness.

Diagnosis	Individual has pressures on him outside work of a nature sufficient to affect his work performance.
Prescription	Explore what can be done to allow individual to cope, including the work demands, and explore the extent of the legitimate involvement of the organization in the life of the individual.
Action	Take up the work manifestations of problems with the individual with a view to working out jointly how he can best be helped and best help himself.
Evaluation	Over time monitor withdrawal from work symptoms.

(f) Role-Role

Some Typical Symptoms	Role conflict, interpersonal conflict, muddled communication, refusal to accept responsibility, work not done.
Diagnosis	Overlapping roles leading to duplication of effort, missing roles, role separation.
Prescription	Re-allocation of tasks and roles, create new roles.
Action	Do re-allocation via new job description, training, recruitment, transfer.
Evaluation	Look for evidence of elimination of presenting symptom.

(g) Role-Group

Some Typical Symptoms	Isolation of the individual. Perceived conflict between individual and a group. Leadership problems. Management style.
Diagnosis	The role of the individual is not perceived as relevant to the needs of the group, (e.g., the introduction of a work study man).
Prescription	Make the needs of the group congruent with the role an individual in that group is required to play (or vice versa).
Action	Make the relevance of the role understood to all concerned by, for example, a clear statement of objectives and discussion of the relevance of the objectives.
Evaluation	Check whether conflict of a disruptive kind is still present.

Individual shows signs of being lost, of incompetence, of isolation, of anxiety. Individual depends on his relationships rather than on job performance.

The role an individual has is not seen as relevant to the requirements of the organization (e.g. the man who has been doing the same job for many years and is now holding up needed change; or the man who has developed in his job in a way not seen as relevant to the objectives of the organization).

Diagnosis

Take steps to re-align the role with the organization, looking for possible adaptation in both.

Prescription

Constructively re-deploy the man whose skills are out of date either within another part of the organization, or find him a job outside. Look at organization objectives to see whether they can be genuinely broadened to include a man's useful but apparently tangential skills.

Action

Check on performance and satisfaction of man, and performance of organization.

Evaluation

An individual is not working effectively, is apparently not interested in work.

The individual is unable to relate 'comfortably' what he is expected to do in his work, with his non-work life (e.g. his job may be very much a cog in a machine, or he may be concerned with making 'anti-social' products: nerve gas, defoliants, etc.)

Diagnosis

Explore possibilities of making a meaningful connection between job and outside world.

Prescription

By means of discussions and change programmes increase the individual's awareness of the value of his role. If this is not possible, remove him from the job.

Action

Check on the performance and attitude of the man.

Evaluation

Lack of co-operation between groups, tasks not being done to schedule, intergroup conflict, 'passing the buck', special problems with specified departments.

(j) Group-Group
*Some Typical
Symptoms*
79

Diagnosis	Difficulties exist in the relationship between two groups because they:

> —see each other as incompetent,
> —they are destructively competing with each other.

Prescription	Explore reasons for perceived incompetence and/or competition. Test certain hypotheses, e.g. B sees A as incompetent because A never gives B information which B needs. A is unable to do this because it does not get the necessary information from Z, but B does not know this; or A deliberately withholds information from B in order to increase its power position, and A is doing this because for some reason it is threatened.
Action	Embark upon sensitivity training type events focusing on the relationships between groups, making sure that the various pictures each has of the other are openly discussed and mutually understood. Encourage groups to work on ways of overcoming their relationship problems including exploring solutions which are specifically technical in nature (e.g. installing certain hardware to ensure that A can give B the information which it requires).
Evaluation	Follow up the ways in which the groups concerned are working, including possibly an assessment of attitude towards other groups.

(k) Group-Organization

Some Typical Symptoms	Strikes, go slows, perceived irrelevance of the headquarters and of certain departments.
Diagnosis	There is a difference between the perceived objectives of the group and the organization, leading to the group not functioning effectively in terms of the organization.
Prescription	Explore the reason for the difference in objectives, why this should be so, what has led to it, and what can be done about it.
Action	Design events, (e.g., workshops) which put on the table the perceived differences in objectives and 'negotiate' a solution (which may mean both sides compromising).
Evaluation	Observe the subsequent relationship between the group and the organization, especially looking for manifestations of differences in perceived 'task'. Include possibly an attitude assessment.

80

Resistance to change, collective absenteeism.

The group is very closely knit in a way which has a negative effect on the organization's objectives owing to influences arising from factors outside work. Working together as a group reinforces their extra-work unity. Such factors unifying the group outside work could be, for example, government policy, or membership of sporting and social activities. Resistance to change would arise, for example, if the closely knit nature of this group at work was threatened by a reorganization.

Diagnosis

Make sure that the group knows that the organization is experiencing the environment's pressure on the group's work as a negative one. Try to explore solutions which may well include a disbandment of the work group.

Prescription

Design events which will lead to the opening up of this conflict in order to allow for the next stage of exploration of solutions. If all fails consider disbanding the group.

Action

Check for presence or absence of symptoms.

Evaluation

In a group of companies a subsidiary is looked upon as not being very effective, and as being poorly run, not meeting various objectives, etc.

**(m) Organization-
Organization**
*Some Typical
Symptoms*

The subsidiary is clearly not achieving the group objectives, but the reasons for this may cover a wide range of possibilities, which would have to be tested. Some are:

Diagnosis

—the subsidiary is not clear what its objectives are;
—there are interpersonal (communication) problems between the managers of the company;
—the subsidiary is genuinely being badly managed;
—the subsidiary knows its objectives but finds them impossible to attain due to factors outside its control, but the company does not appreciate this;
—the set objectives are unrealistic.

It is essential that all relevant people get together to explore the above issues.

Prescription

81

Action	Bring about such an exploration; making sure its objectives are clearly understood by all so that they are not forced to be always on the defensive and hence unreceptive. Such an event would again have a sensitivity training atmosphere about it, as it would probably involve a certain amount of interpersonal confrontation.
Evaluation	Check on performance of subsidiary, and on the quality of the relationship between the subsidiary and the company.

(n) Organization-Environment

Some Typical Symptoms	Organization fails; loses customers; is full of destructive internal conflict; profit margins drop although turnover increases, etc.
Diagnosis	In some way or another the organization has failed to adapt to changing environmental conditions.
Prescription	The reasons for this failure to adapt have to be explained, and the sort of things to look for include:

—signs of rigidity in the organized structure, when the environment is demanding an increasingly flexible response;
—too much power and responsibility concentrated in too few areas, leading to impossibly demanding jobs for some and very undemanding jobs for others;
—wrong decisions being taken by the organization's top management, leading to decreasing viability;
—failure to develop the human resources of the organization so that the necessary talent is not available in sufficient quantities;
—lack of long-term capital investments so that an organization cannot re-equip itself to cope with changing technologies.

Action	There is no simple action, as so many interests are involved, but some of the things which could be done include:

—a reappraisal of the organization's business so that it knows what need it is fulfilling in the market place; this will provide the reference point for appraising the relevance of the tasks which are going on in the organization, and this in turn will lead to changing tasks and changing roles;
—an expansion of the human resources (personnel) function so that much more money is invested in people in the form of training at all levels; this will ensure that people are equipped to cope with the new tasks. Such training will not

only cover new technical skills, but will also usually involve learning about how to cope with increased authority, responsibility and autonomy.

—the setting up of information systems so that managers have more facts on which to base their decisions.

Check to see whether the organization has found viability. (N.B. Sometimes when confronted with considerable change the viability of an organization apparently gets worse before it gets better.)

Evaluation

Within the context of diagnosis of an organization's problems this interface is not usually a useful one to explore. It is valid in terms of exploring differences between the environment as it is *perceived* by an organization, and as it really is, as organizations act on their perception of the environment.

(o) Environment-Environment

These relationships then give an indication of the breadth of possible behavioural science applications. The following chapters develop some of these relationships further by a closer look at leadership, group relations training, job design, and organizational development.

8
Leadership

Leadership is not as simple as many assume; it has been the subject of extended discussion, research, and argument for many years. Moreover the emotive connotations of the word have brought it into some disrepute in a society of increasingly egalitarian and anti-militaristic values. But the process of influencing the behaviour of others in varying degrees and by various means exists today, as it always has. Equality and democracy do not eliminate influence and leadership, but they change the means by which it may be accomplished. This is important inasmuch as it generates changed expectations about participation, involvement, consultation and representation among those with whom the manager has to work. The manager's means of influencing the behaviour of others must alter correspondingly. Among those who say that people's loyalty and discipline are not what they used to be, there exists the need to recognize that in a situation of changed socio-economic values their techniques of influence and leadership may no longer be appropriate.

Is it possible to change a person's style of leadership? Surely leaders are born and not made? There are no 'yes' or 'no' answers. If there is an answer, it is that it all depends on the circumstances and on the individual. Certainly, for many people, changing their behaviour is difficult, and in some cases it is impossible. Only small modifications in an individual's sensitivity to others, his ability to communicate, his receptiveness to the ideas of others, may be possible.

The individual may find himself in, or indeed may actually seek, an environment which constantly reinforces his normal pattern of leadership behaviour; this then becomes incorporated into his self-image, frequently rendering change almost impossible, particularly in middle and later life.

Against this background, some of the attempts to train for social, interpersonal and leadership skills must be regarded as naive, ignoring as they sometimes do the influence of the environment, and many years of repeated learning. Manipulation of specific items in an individual's behaviour repertoire, in a non-real environment, is unlikely to be effective.

It is also the case that some qualities and aptitudes with which we are born, which we acquire early in life, will subsequently influence and support our attempts at leader behaviour. High intelligence, articulateness and determination are qualities which we might agree are 'useful' in leadership situations; indeed there is some research evidence to support the contention that qualities and aptitudes of a certain kind are important to leadership. Cattell[1] notes that in research carried out into personality, intelligence, and leadership in small face-to-face groups there were some significant common traits among those *elected* as leaders. These were:

(a) elected leaders are significantly above average intelligence;
(b) they are higher in traits such as emotional maturity, persistence, conscientiousness and extroversion.

But one must be cautious about the 'qualities' approach. Many research projects have been carried out to discover if successful leadership has a relationship to personality traits. Over the past fifty years there have been hundreds of studies made comparing physical, intellectual and personality traits of leaders with their successfulness in life. These studies usually come up with a list of traits that made for 'good' leadership. But on the whole this approach has been disappointing. Only five per cent of the traits in over one hundred studies appeared in four or more of them.

The investigations indicated that a variety of persons with different personality, environmental, and educational backgrounds could make successful leaders. Opportunity must also be important and holding a leadership position over a long period might be partly responsible for developing the traits. Moreover, the 'static' qualities of leaders do not help in understanding the *process* of leadership, or the extent to which different situations call forth different qualities and different 'styles'.

Another issue to be considered is that different styles are seen as variously good or bad. While it may generally be true that in the present day a consultative, democratic, problem-solving style may be more effective than a straight autocratic command in dealing with subordinates, this has to be qualified by saying that much depends on the nature of the situation and the task which requires leadership. It is obvious that to some extent the nature of the situation influences the way in which people *expect* to be led. In an emergency situation, or in one where there is little doubt about who has the expertise to deal with the problem, a consultative approach might be regarded as incompetent and timid.

The operation of 'fail-dangerous' equipment, (e.g., aircraft, or services engaged in crisis management) tends to call for extremely direct and autocratic management. The factors of control and speed of operation dictate a clear chain of command and little consultative problem solving. Here, however, care must be taken not to assume that following autocratically laid-down behaviour specifications lead to non-harmonious relationships and disaffected people. Aircrew may enjoy extremely egalitarian and harmonious relationships, recognizing none the less the distinctive roles to be performed according to a rigidly laid down schedule. An important point is that standards of behaviour in a highly programmed task may have been the subject of representative discussions. These situations promote the development of a distinctive hierarchy of competence, easily recognizable by badges of rank. The rank is accepted as an immediate indication of competence and authority, since the situation will not provide the opportunity for that competence to be tested out and for the relative merits of the way in which the task may be carried out, to be discussed.

At the other end of the scale will be found groups whose objectives and goals are not clear (perhaps even to the members), and whose different competences and contributions to achieving the task are understood only informally. Here the degree of influence a member will exercise may have evolved over time—as the competences have been steadily observed by the group—and accepted. The leadership of the group may shift from individual to individual as different tasks and problems arise within the group, and it may be extremely difficult to recognize consistent individual degrees of influence, except in so far as they emerge in specific situations.

Different ways of thinking about leadership have been implicit in the above. It can be thought of as:

> an attribute of an office (e.g. a position)
> a sum of various qualities,
> or a category or style of behaviour.

But leadership involves the use of authority in making decisions. Authority is legitimate power, power held by the consent of those over whom it is exercised; but the source of legitimacy or consent is obviously variable. Usually, legitimate power rests on the basis of:

- expertise, a technical competence;
- a function of office, the possession of rewards and sanctions;
- personal qualities, power of persuasion and communication, etc. (including status/prestige brought in from outside the group);
- the manner in which the authority is exercised.

It is clear from these sources of legitimacy that management depends on all four, but according to the task and situation, the *validity* of the sources, their strength in legitimizing the use of power, may vary. Awareness of all four sources, and an understanding of their use, is important in considering management behaviour.

It is interesting to examine some of the models and theories of leadership and management styles developed by behavioural scientists.

LEADER STYLE AND SUBORDINATE MOTIVATION

Douglas McGregor in his celebrated work *The Human Side of Enterprise*[2] argued that the style of management adopted by a manager was a function of his assumptions about people. Although the extent to which the task influences styles of management and leadership was not accounted for, this was an important contribution which initiated much discussion and research into the relative effectiveness of different approaches to influencing subordinate behaviour. It has of course special relevance to changing social values and employment conditions. McGregor's theories X and Y represent polar assumptions about work and people. They are:

THEORY X	THEORY
(1) Work is inherently distasteful to most people.	Work is as natural as play if the conditions are favourable.
(2) Most people are not ambitious, have little desire for responsibility and prefer to be directed.	Self-control is often indispensable in achieving organizational goals.
(3) Most people have little capacity for creativity in solving organizational problems.	The capacity for creativity in solving organizational problems is widely distributed in the population.
(4) Motivation occurs only at the physiological and security levels.	Motivation occurs at the affiliation, esteem and self-actualization levels, as well as physiological and security levels.
(5) Most people must be closely controlled and often coerced to achieve organizational objectives.	People can be self-directed and creative at work if properly motivated.

87

Theory X then, assumes that most people prefer to be directed, do not want responsibility, and above all desire security. Money, fringe benefits and fear of punishment determine performance.

Theory Y paints another view of man—that man can be basically self-directing, creative, responsible, and that work does not for most people constitute a necessary evil. The rewards that motivate to achieve high work performance are the rewards of affiliation, self-esteem, prestige and self-actualization. McGregor's theories, or more accurately categories of assumptions, are derived from Maslow[3] and the 'growth-fulfilment' school of motivation theory (see chapter 4), and their orientation to the improvement of work performance. Fig. 8.1 illustrates the changing style of leadership appropriate as one moves from an X to a Y type organization.

McGregor and others who have followed him (Argyris[4], Likert[5], and Bennis[6]) have advocated alternative management styles which, on the whole, allow for satisfactions to be derived from work of a 'higher' order than had hitherto been considered. While perhaps much of their work may appear evangelical in

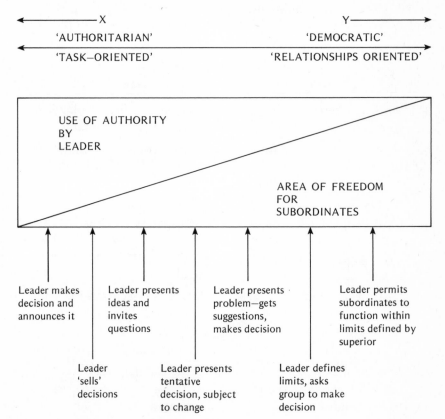

Fig. 8.1 *Leadership style and organizational culture*

nature, it is based on the awareness of changing social values in society, which themselves affect the climate of control within which many people want to work. In the final analysis the question is of *control*, and the degree of control operated by one person over another. Different situations will give rise to different *control needs*, and different personalities will have varying requirements as to their need to *control*: the extent to which they feel able to trust, and tolerate ambiguity; and their need to *be controlled*: level of competence, degree of 'self-sufficiency', etc.

Rensis Likert[5] takes the standpoint that effective management means effective human resources management, and from research done in 200 or more firms he developed a model of four systems of organization.

THE HUMAN ORGANIZATION

SYSTEM 1	SYSTEM 2	SYSTEM 3	SYSTEM 4
Exploitive Authoritative	Benevolent Authoritative	Consultative	Participative Group

Each of these systems has structural/behavioural characteristics which determine the nature of leadership processes. They all have different:

> motivational forces
> communication processes
> interaction and influence
> decision-making processes
> goal-setting
> control processes

By questionnaire, over a sample of management, it is possible to establish an organization's general approach to the co-ordination and control of work effort. Likert's major contention is that System 4, resting on the principles of supportive relationships, group methods of supervision, involvement in work-related decisions, and delegation of responsibility, is a more effective system of management than the others. This is supported by his research findings. Here are some of the questions which Likert asked to determine the organization 'style':

> How free do subordinates feel to talk to superiors about job?
> Where is responsibility felt for achieving organization's goals?
> How is downward communication accepted?
> How well do superiors know problems faced by subordinates?
> Are subordinates involved in decisions related to their work?
> How are organizational goals established?
> What are cost, productivity, and other control data used for?

Likert's research suggests that System 4 management probably has wide applicability. He says,

> The nature of the specific procedures for applying System 4 management in a particular firm will vary depending on the nature of the work and the traditions of the company. The basic principles of System 4 management . . . are the same, however, for all situations.

Although Likert tends to talk about 'systems' as if they related to a fundamental set of rules, such rules, which of course influence the way in which people behave, are themselves thought up, enforced, and managed by people. Hence, his four systems reflect leadership styles which arise from varying behavioural assumptions made by management. Throughout an organization these assumptions give rise to varying degrees of constraint on people's behaviour affecting for example:

when and how they communicate,
who makes decisions,
how performance is controlled,
the degree of competitiveness in groups,
the degree of co-operation between groups,
the strength of identity with company goals.

Likert's work rests squarely on the assumption that leadership, to be effective, must aim to stimulate motivation through participation and involvement.

JOB CONTENT AND MOTIVATION

In chapter 4 motivation and work were discussed, and these, clearly, are central to any discussion of leadership. Leadership is concerned with motivating people to an appropriate level of performance. The emphasis placed on *job content* factors in meeting higher level needs is very relevant in appreciating leadership.

The evidence from those, such as Herzberg[7] and Trist[8], who have looked at job content, suggests that effective management style depends on considerations additional to the correct treatment of people. The nature of the task itself has critical implications for the extent to which an individual can become self-motivating and controlling. At a simple level a boss manages a man, and a man manages his task. No matter how excellent the boss's management may be, if the man's task is intrinsically boring and dull, then there will be leadership problems. This situation probably occurs frequently, but the opposite can also happen. A man's task may be intrinsically interesting and fulfilling, but his boss may be an incompetent manager. Again leadership problems will arise.

If the leader's job is to motivate his group in the direction of co-operatively achieving a task, such motivation will not only be a matter of facilitating good relationships between members of the group, but will also demand *facilitating a good relationship between the individual and his work.*

A number of theories have been discussed which, with their focus on motivation, have obvious relevance for management and leadership. It is necessary now to consider individual differences in expectations about being led. Such differences are practical considerations in any management situation. Will everyone respond to some of the 'prescribed' styles? In studies carried out in the USA, M. Scott Myers[9] was able to distinguish between two distinctive groups when using Herzberg's model. *'Motivation Seekers'* are influenced primarily by the task itself—are 'inner directed'—and can tolerate a high degree of poor-environment factors. *'Maintenance Seekers'*, on the other hand, are affected primarily by the nature of their environment and are generally pre-occupied and dissatisfied with job factors, such as pay, supplementary benefits, type of supervision, working conditions, etc. These groups have been described as 'outer-directed'. Most significant of Scott Myers' findings have been that although an individual's orientation as a motivation-seeker, or maintenance-seeker, has some permanence, it can be influenced by the working group, which will tend to get the individual, whatever his orientation, to adopt group standards.

This suggests that to operate effectively as a leader means operating within a group context. An attempt to be a more effective leader with any one individual must be made in the light of two considerations:

- the extent to which group norms control individual behaviour,
- the role which the individual and the group expect the leader to play (i.e. the role which is 'offered' to the leader).

In an ongoing situation a leader is concerned with meeting several needs. He must meet the demands of the task or goal, but in order to do this he must also pay close attention to the needs of the group, and to the needs of the individual. A leader's job is to balance these needs. Leadership is an activity, whether the authority is based upon 'office', a 'preferred style', or 'personal

LEADERSHIP
AS AN
ONGOING
ACTIVITY

qualities', and the activity is essentially aimed at achieving a goal—this is why the group exists. Whatever the group goal is, certain actions have to be taken in order to reach it. Certain activities have to be provided by and for the group members. Activities for achieving the task include:

> stating the problem
> initiating plans and decisions
> giving opinions (sifting information and directions)
> co-ordinating efforts
> suggesting solutions
> developing methods
> evaluating progress

Goal-oriented activities alone however are not enough. In most cases, for instance, it would be harmful if only a few members of the group arrived at the intended goal, or the goal was reached only at the price of the disintegration of the group. Not many organizations can afford to solve their problems at the expense of their own destruction. Functions have to be provided therefore which help to maintain the group as a social entity. (Likert's notions of supportive behaviour, involvement, etc., are aimed at this). Functions of this work include:

> participation in decision-making,
> acceptance (or at least tolerance) of others' opinions,
> combining ideas of members and mediating conflict,
> channelling potentially destructive individual behaviour into constructive efforts,
> facilitating the communication process,
> developing trust (the first sign of distrust among people is the withholding of information).

Group maintenance functions ideally should aim to create a climate in which group members can participate in such a way that their own interests and competences can be effectively identified with, and utilized for, the purposes of the group.

Members of groups have individual as well as group needs. Individual needs will have their source of satisfaction in the expression of individual behaviour within the group, and will include desires such as wanting to obtain prestige, to belong, receive approval, etc. Other needs will be concerned with the nature of the work itself, e.g., making decisions, accepting responsibility, learning, etc. The leader's job is to facilitate as much expression and satisfaction of individual needs within the group as is compatible with other's needs, with group maintenance and with task achievement.

	THE TASK	THE GROUP	THE INDIVIDUAL
Effect of *Task* needs on (for example)		*Nature of Technology* employed will influence structure of: (a) Relationships and co-operation (b) Communications (c) Status system (d) Job context factors (e) External evaluation of the job (f) Controls which have to be exercised	Help determine: (a) Job content and 'intrinsic' satisfaction (b) Individual status in group (c) Individual status outside group (d) Life cycle/style outside work (e) Monetary earnings
Effect of *Group* needs on (for example)	(a) Degree of co-operation affects task (b) Group may amend task (c) Group norms on output (d) Skill "mix" and deployment (e) Competition with other work groups		Provides: (a) Membership (b) Social support (c) Recognition (d) Status Requiring: Behaviour standards
Effect of *Individual* needs on (for example)	(a) Individual knowledge and skills (b) Other 'personal qualities' (c) If frustrated may mean lower individual productivity	(a) Express self— e.g. status needs, idiosyncratic behaviour (b) Compatibility with other team members (c) Ability to contribute to group standards (d) Level of expertise, etc.	

Fig. 8.2 *Some interactions between task, group, and individual requirements*

The interacting nature of task, group and individual needs can be very complex. The matrix in Fig. 8.2 sets out a number of these interactions.

From Fig. 8.2 some of the skills relevant to leadership can be suggested.

For example, for task needs a leader should have technical, diagnostic, problem-solving, scheduling, and administrative skills. He should be able to organize and divide labour, establish controls, and evaluate objectives and methods.

For group needs he should have communications and social skills; an ability to diagnose group processes; to facilitate intergroup relationships and co-operation; to mediate conflict; to channel efforts to groups, and to match individuals in task relationships.

SOME
LEADERSHIP
SKILLS

For individual needs he should be able to identify individual needs in a group; identify particular skills; help learning processes; be able to provide supportive behaviour; give feedback on performance; and relate the individual to the task and the group.

These skills are relatively abstract. To make them more concrete, it would be necessary to relate the needs and skills required to a particular job. To make the matter of leadership more difficult still, no one individual probably incorporates all the skills necessary. Personality traits and aptitudes will differentiate individuals in terms of their competence for certain situations, hence in examining the question of leadership for any one job, one would also have to examine (in terms of achieving objectives) which dimension presents the greatest problem, and which special abilities one would seek. Many organizations tend to seek task-related skills, when looking for a leader, when an assessment of the *real* problem of leadership in the situation might suggest other more needed skills in the area of group and individual needs.

One of the main characteristics about the work on leadership styles has been the tendency to assume that a certain style of leadership (System 4, Theory Y, participative, or employee-centred) tends to be 'better' than all the others. There is some evidence for this. Likert did some research to discover the general pattern of management used by high producing managers in contrast to that used by other managers. He found that

> supervisors with the best records of performance focus their primary attention on the human aspects of their subordinates' problems and on endeavouring to build effective work groups with high performance goals.

These supervisors were called 'employee-centred' and were found to have high producing sections.

Argyle[10] reports that a considerable number of comparisons have been carried out on the effect of autocratic and democratic style in leadership, both in the USA and in Britain.

> The main finding is that democratic leaders ... are more effective both in terms of productivity or effectiveness variables, and in terms of high job satisfaction, low labour turnover and low absenteeism.

The main reason why the democratic style is generally more effective is that influencing and organizing people with consideration for them as people, tends to create a social obligation to reciprocate by complying with requests. Participation in decision making tends to create a higher level of commitment to the task, and democratic discussion facilitates communication and cohesion in the group. It also brings the group pressure of a collective decision to bear on task performance. It generates helping relationships in which the ideas and talents of individuals may become known and used by the group. Research carried out by Sadler[11] among managers indicates a general preference for a consultative style of management and leadership, a style which was correlated with high job satisfaction. An important implication of this research was that a large proportion of the research sample valued *consistency* in style, as much as any particular style.

Many changes in the nature of work have supported the movement towards more democratic forms of management and leadership. Indeed this change is being 'forced' on some management—it is by no means a function of management's initiative. Many employers have sought to extend the degree of their control over the work situation, only to encounter resistance to this autocratic, directive and non-participative style of leadership. Management generally has reduced its control over employee behaviour in the years since the Second World War. This is a process which appears to be national as well as organizational, and has its roots in the socio-economic changes and in communications technology. This reduction indicates the importance of recognizing that organizations are not entities separated from society; what is happening in the outside world must be taken into account.

Many forms of training which seek to change leadership style are perceived as 'progressive' or even as 'radical' innovations—indeed, this is the image preferred by the developers of these 'tools'. In reality they may be simply the means by which an organization makes a somewhat tardy response to the problems and pressures of its functioning, and even then only a partial response.

Leadership is itself behaviour, and as has been stated, behaviour is a function of the *personality* and the *situation*.

Much leadership training is an attempt to change relatively peripheral aspects of personality, knowledge, attitudes, conceptions. However, leadership training can make few changes to situations, which themselves may in part be dictated by market or technological considerations. To provide more democratic/participative styles of leadership, means also providing the *structure* (the framework of authority and controls) in an organization which encourages and reinforces this form of leadership behaviour. Failure to do so has left many organizations (especially some of the most well known 'institutional preachers' of democratic/participative management style) with a difficult gap between the 'words' and the action—between the spoken ideal, and reality.

This is a complex problem. Some of the desired changes in structure may not be possible—financial and operational reasons usually placing important constraints. Also, the learning about leadership has not really changed the way in which the manager experiences his environment; he *knows* the need to act differently, but he does *not understand* it as an 'internal' imperative. In this critical area of relationships with people who have interpersonal skills, defence mechanisms, deep-rooted attitudes to people, to punishment, or reward, change is neither easy nor lightly undertaken.

SUMMARY

The desire to have an ideal type of leader is common. Even now writers in the field of leadership tend to emphasise some desirable style. The typical stereotype of leadership is one which suggests doing things *to* and *for* people rather than *with* them. In fact, the problem of influencing others' behaviour in the direction of achieving a task is subtle, and different tasks in different situations generate different leadership patterns. Today, with rapidly changing social values, a constant revision of the ways of thinking about management and leadership is essential.

REFERENCES

(1) Cattell, R. B., *The Scientific Analysis of Personality*, Penguin, 1965.
(2) McGregor, D., *The Human Side of Enterprise*, New York: McGraw-Hill, 1960.
(3) Maslow, A. H., *Motivation and Personality*, New York: Harper Row, 1954.
(4) Argyris, C., *Integrating the Individual and the Organization*, New York: Wiley, 1964.
(5) Likert, R. L., *The Human Organization: Its Management and Value*, New York: McGraw-Hill, 1967.
(6) Bennis, W. G., *Changing Organizations*, New York: McGraw-Hill, 1967.
(7) Herzberg, F., *Work and the Nature of Man*, Cleveland and New York: World Publishing Co., 1966.
(8) Trist, E. L., Higgin, G. W., Murray, H., and Pollock, A. B., *Organizational Choice: Capabilities of Groups at the Coal Face Under Changing Technologies*, Tavistock Publications, 1963.

(9) Scott-Myers, M., 'Who are your motivated workers?' *Harvard Business Review*, **42,** 1, 1964.

(10) Argyle, M., *Social Interaction*, Methuen, 1969.

(11) Sadler, P. J., 'Leadership style, confidence in management, and job satisfaction', *Journal of Applied Behavioral Science*, **6,** 1970, pp. 1-19.

9
Group relations training

Group relations training is the commonly accepted name to cover many terms which managers will have encountered: T-groups, sensitivity training, human relations training, and managerial grids. This chapter is intended to convey an appreciation of why this type of training exists, why it is sometimes regarded as controversial and what forms it frequently takes.

There are two important factors to be considered when describing the context of group relations training.

CHANGES IN LEARNING

The first concerns the increased understanding about the way people learn. Growing economic wealth, increased standards of education, the impact of mass communication—especially television—are leading to a gradual modification of the traditional master/student relationship. This traditional relationship is put under considerable pressure today by the increasing rate of discovery, specialization, and change in both values and knowledge about learning. It is easy for the master to get out of date, and keeping in touch means greater specialization, with growing emphasis on the master integrating the 'self'-learning of the pupils. He becomes less authoritative and more consultative. No longer can he be even one jump ahead of his class for much of the time. Learning itself is tending to become far more democratic and involving. Children at school are increasingly encouraged to find out for themselves rather than be told, and the 'discovering' method of learning appears, for many applications, to be more effective; certainly it is more rewarding for the learner. The traditional method of learning is essentially an intellectual process, where having a good memory is a virtue. 'Finding out for yourself' learning, in addition to being an intellectual process, engages other mental processes as well, indeed it engages the emotions and, as a result of this, the learner becomes more involved in what he is learning. Furthermore, such learning is less 'prescriptive', it enables the student to determine more for himself 'what is' and 'what should be' through his senses, rather than hear through the teacher.

Slowly but surely, then, learning methods are changing,

especially in primary schools, but also in secondary schools and universities. Increasingly, *employers will be dealing with people at all levels who seek to learn in a way different from that of their organizational superiors.* This will cause, indeed is causing, stresses and strains on 'the system' as it, itself, must change in order to cope.

The second consideration concerns how people go about seeking solutions to difficulties. At most levels in organizations, people find themselves dealing with problems. The conventional approach for problem solving is to define the problem, and then set about solving it by arranging, as far as possible, for the information necessary to be available. Having done this a decision will be taken, usually by one person. This method has worked well in the past, especially if the problems are more or less isolated and independent of other concerns. Today, however, people find themselves trying to handle an environment where problems are not easily defined and are not isolated, but are complex and interrelated. Emery[1] gives an example of how complex environments can effect a more or less conventional investment decision. A pea canning firm decided to invest in a new pea canning factory, but failed to forsee the many environmental influences which led to an irreversible change in market conditions and subsequent failure of the investment. These factors included imported fruits, post-war controls on steel strip, developments in quick-freezing, surplus crops not suitable for quick-freezing, animal feed, agricultural exports by under-developed countries, own-branding, growth of supermarkets, greater variety of vegetable products, and more small canning firms. Such complexity cannot be effectively handled by isolated problem solving.

Man's changing needs, the change in ways of learning and the move from *isolated problem solving* to *complex solution seeking* are all seen as providing a 'ground' against which group relations training has emerged as a significant 'figure'.

If people are to work together, particularly in complex solution-seeking, in a way which is effective in terms of the task and also self-fulfilling, they must appreciate and use their own interdependence. This means that they must know and accept each others' strengths and weaknesses, and learn ways of handling individual and group issues, such as authority and conflict. When a group has achieved such a level of interpersonal openness, it can proceed much more effectively with its task. Many of us are familiar with the way tasks can be held up because of 'personality' problems: people refusing to talk to each other, information being withheld, etc., and how individuals are apparently unable to see alternative ways of playing their managerial role, and have set ideas about and ways of perceiving the world of work*. Group relations training is a technique for enabling people to examine these issues, to develop diagnostic skills, and acquire new interpersonal approaches.

The nucleus of all training of this kind are the small groups usually referred to as T-groups. (The 'T' stands for training.) A T-group usually numbers about eight people and includes a trainer who is qualified in psychology or one of its associated disciplines (clinical psychology, psychiatry, or psycho-analysis). Group relations training events range from the small group meeting once a week for about ten weeks, to several groups attending a residential training 'laboratory', where there are events in addition to the T-group work. These residential laboratories usually last one or two weeks but occasionally may last for three months.

In the T-group itself, the group, with the trainer, will meet for periods of usually about one and a half hours. There is no fixed agenda for discussion, but most participants will have some idea of what they are there for, through prior publicity and information.

Typically, discussion focuses on problems of interpersonal communication, and will vary from neutral to 'loaded' topics. The trainer's role is to aid the group in coping with its own problems of communication, and because of this the role is a controversial one. The trainer will often, in the eyes of the group, seem to make things difficult, uncertain and unnecessarily complex.

In a typical group relations training laboratory, sessions other than T-groups will include events where all those attending can discuss what is happening, where what they are learning from the T-groups can be evaluated, where problems of working as a temporary 'community' are aired, where problem-solving 'games' are played. Particular attention is paid to relating the laboratory learning to 'real life'. This is not easy, but the impact of individuals' feelings on situations are part of everyday life. Increasingly, these issues need to be taken into account, for the reasons discussed earlier, and group relations training provides a 'safe' environment in which they can be examined. By intellectual and more importantly, experiential exploration, members of a

* An absorbing account of interpersonal difficulties in a real life situation, the story of the discovery of the molecular structure of DNA is told in *The Double Helix*[2].

T-group will find themselves learning about a variety of 'human' situations. Some examples are given below, but it must be emphasized that these examples do not provide a comprehensive summary of all that occurs in a T-group.

'When you said A, I thought you meant B'.

(a) Difficulties in communications

The opportunity arises not only to work out what misunderstandings occur, but why they occur. The 'why' can be difficult to deal with because people find themselves looking at their perceptions of other people, and other people's perceptions of them. For example, if X dislikes Y he will hear a message from Y different from the one he would hear if he liked Y. Problems of communication of this kind commonly arise between:

    people of noticeably different personalities;
    the sexes;
    different age groups;
    different 'disciplines';
    different 'perceived statuses'.

The increasing emphasis on people working as members of groups in organizations begin to reveal how important and how difficult it is to establish effective communication.

(b) Competition and Co-operation

Arising from the communication problem are problems of competing and co-operating. To work effectively, groups in organizations should co-operate, yet individual differences encourage competition. A T-group will often explore the impact of co-operation on the individual, in that the individual will have to relinquish some of his own power and control if he is to co-operate.

(c) Leadership

Following on from the above, groups generally provide themselves with a leader, and the leader remains as long as the group want him to, or as long as he can impose himself on the group. Different leaders are valuable for different situations and therefore the problem of changing a leader will arise. In competitive groups, this is often stressful because a leader being removed is a 'loser'. In a co-operative group, changes of leadership are achieved in a more 'problem solving' way without the need for anyone to 'lose out'.

(d) Feelings

The movement towards increasing an individual's participation and involvement in work implies that more of an individual is being engaged than just his ability to carry out a prescribed set of actions. 'Employing the whole man' is a term which is becoming increasingly used, and what this means can be explored in group relations training. For example, an appreciation can be gained of how a person's feelings and emotions can influence his contributions to the group; how his feelings about other people, and other people's feelings about him can also be appreciated in terms of his contribution to the group. People often go to work in a bad mood, and it would be valuable to them to have some idea of how their mood influences their actions at work, and hence other people.

(e) Learning

Learning by finding out is well demonstrated in group relations training as individuals explore each other's reaction to situations, and tackle problems. Group relations training events can and often do combine 'pure' T-group work with more structured problem-solving activities so that people can appreciate the different approaches to problem solving. Such T-groups, which can be described as task-centred, endeavour to relate the T-group learning and experience to concrete problem-solving activities, so that the interaction of one with the other can be demonstrated.

PEOPLE CREATE ENVIRONMENTS

Behaviour is the result of a relationship between the individual with his 'personality' and the environment he is in. Personality is the outcome of inherited characteristics and experiences in life, and people with different personalities will react to the same situation in different ways. These are important points to remember in the work environment as, for example, apparently disruptive behaviour on the part of an individual can be either the result of his personality, or because of the situation in which he finds himself. The interplay between the personality and the environment ranges along a spectrum from one end, where certain environmental conditions will cause many different personalities to behave in more or less the same way (for example, a football crowd); to the other end where a given environmental condition will give rise to a great range of behaviour. In an organization it would be of great value to know what effect the environment has on behaviour, although this is not easy to determine. All too easily do people find themselves explaining the behaviour of others in personality terms alone.

The simple definition of behaviour in the above paragraph is only a starting point and needs further elaboration. *People help to create environments.* If a manager plays his role according to the beliefs which he has about people which are of an authoritarian kind ('theory X') then he is likely to generate conditions in his own work environment which will seem to confirm his beliefs, i.e. that people have to be handled in an authoritarian manner.

Litwin and Stringer[3] explored the relationship between work motivation and organizational climate. Organizational climate was found to be extremely determining in the kinds of motivation aroused in employees. Three major motivations, the need for achievement, the need for power, and the need for affiliation, were found to be differentially aroused according to the different strengths of certain features which collectively made up the 'climate' of the organization. These features included the degree of constraint and structure in the enterprise, the different emphasis on reward and punishment, the presence or otherwise of supportive and encouraging relationships, the emphasis on individual responsibility, and the perceived performance standards set by management. In turn, all these features of organizational climate were highly influenced by the leadership style of the management. Evidently, therefore, the perceptions and assumptions which managers have of their environment (which includes other people and their needs) will affect critically their behaviour and in consequence the behaviour (and hence lives) of others.

Group relations training is used to explore values, assumptions and perceptions, and their impact on the behaviour of others. The tasks which people are asked to carry out, however, also have a very important effect on behaviour (see chapter 5).

Technologies are usually designed in ignorance of their effect on the relations between people and groups, and in job satisfaction and motivation. Group relations training is sometimes carried out in ignorance of the way in which technology and administrative systems inevitably structure roles and constrain behaviour. Faced with these influences, attempts to change, for example, leadership style and interpersonal skills, may have only a marginal effect. Indeed, if the individual acquires a new 'style' of behaviour, and new values and perceptions, and then returns to work where the normal pattern of role expectations exists, he is likely to find himself non-conforming, and thereby under some stress.

However, if a situation exists of working difficulties within and between groups, of inadequate communications, hostilities and irrational assumptions, where is the starting point for even considering new organization and role structures which will assist in modifying such dysfunctional activities? A start must be made somewhere, and not infrequently it is valuable to explore by means of group relations training: values and attitudes; the perceptions held of other people's needs; the desire for rational interpretations of behaviour; perceived leadership style, interpersonal competence with subordinates, bosses and peers. It is necessary in fact to examine and thereby modify aspects of behaviour, while bearing in mind the manner in which the task and the technology 'structurally induce' certain patterns of behaviour.

GROUP
RELATIONS
TRAINING IN
INDUSTRY

Group relations training has taken different forms in its development in industry. Figure 9.1 gives an indication of the range of learning situations which come within its broad context.

Depending on the existing 'culture' of the enterprise, the use of group relations training methods vary. The more structured 'workshop' form of training will be less concerned with personal 'insight', while the learning acquired in a T-Group will include: sensitivity to emotional reaction in others and to interpersonal phenomena, in groups and organizations; clearer self-perception; awareness of how an individual is seen by others and greater self-understanding and self-acceptance; learning to behave as a member of a democratic group becoming less dependent on leaders and more accepting of others; better understanding of interpersonal behaviour in groups and organizations; learning how to learn by making use of feedback and seeking the help of others. The objective is, of course, greater individual and group effectiveness in the work situation.

Organizations and employers of the future are going to place a renewed emphasis on human relations and allied skills. This is not

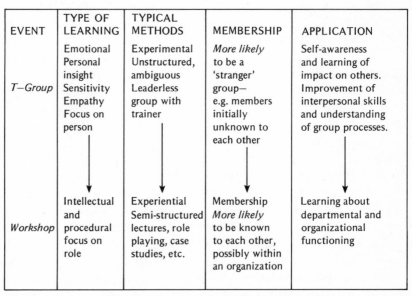

EVENT	TYPE OF LEARNING	TYPICAL METHODS	MEMBERSHIP	APPLICATION
T—Group	Emotional Personal insight Sensitivity Empathy Focus on person	Experimental Unstructured, ambiguous Leaderless group with trainer	*More likely* to be a 'stranger' group— e.g. members initially unknown to each other	Self-awareness and learning of impact on others. Improvement of interpersonal skills and understanding of group processes.
Workshop	Intellectual and procedural focus on role	Experiential Semi-structured lectures, role playing, case studies, etc.	Membership *More likely* to be known to each other, possibly within an organization	Learning about departmental and organizational functioning

Fig. 9.1 *An indication of the variable aspects of Group relations training*

only because of the need to develop and involve people more effectively in their tasks, but also because complex and rapidly changing organizations generate stresses which manifest themselves in the relationships between people and groups which have to be managed. The trend therefore towards in-company team-building exercises, participative change programmes, sensitivity training, and other approaches, is not just 'fashion'. The growing concern to provide environments where individuals and groups can function more effectively is a response by organizations to changing circumstances and will require highly developed skills of consultation, social diagnosis, leadership, communication, and conflict management.

Group relations training is open to abuse. Its use in a directive or manipulative way is wrong and may be damaging to individuals and the organization. The gaining of personal insight, the exploration of values and perceptions, and the learning of diagnostic skills in groups is a highly participative experience. Such learning experiences should develop as part of a programme which allows people to participate in the development of new ideas about organizations, and helps them to assist each other in acquiring new skills to manage them. They should become part of the ongoing life of the enterprise and be the originators of change ideas, rather than be used to manipulate people into the acceptance of new 'creeds' handed down from management.

Its value in helping understanding and in providing insight into organizational change makes group relations training a powerful method. Such methods should not be either ignored or entered into lightly.

REFERENCES

(1) Emery, F. E., and Trist, E. L., 'The Causal Texture of Organizational Environments.' In F. E. Emery (ed.), *Systems thinking*, Penguin, 1969, pp. 241-260.
(2) Watson, J. D., *The Double Helix*, Penguin, 1970.
(3) Litwin, G. H., and Stringer, R. A., *Motivation and Organizational Climate*, Harvard University Press, 1968.

FURTHER READING

Bradford, L. P., Gibb, J. R., and Benne, K. D., (eds.), *T-group Theory and Laboratory Method: Innovation in Re-Education*, New York: Wiley, 1964.
Whitaker, G., (ed.), *T-Group Training: Group Dynamics in Management Education*, Blackwell, 1965.

10
Job design

The practice of job design has traditionally been the preserve of industrial and methods engineers. Indeed the actual work that a man is asked to do is frequently an almost incidental consequence of the way in which the work flow and equipment are designed. The increased awareness of factors affecting people's motivation and performance at work has led to attempts to redesign work to bring about increased performance on the part of the employee largely as a function of the intrinsic rewards arising from the job itself (interest, responsibility, and self-direction). This means that jobs must be changed to allow for such intrinsic rewards. Increasingly, these principles are being applied in the design of new work systems.

A number of job design practices are briefly outlined below.

(a) Job Rotation   This does not involve one job but several. The job-holder changes jobs with others in order to relieve problems arising from certain tasks; for example, tasks of extreme repetition or of extreme accuracy and closeness of work. The job is in fact unchanged, but individuals are rotated around them at certain intervals. Frequently, payment schemes permitting, such rotation is done informally by employees.

(b) Job Enlargement   A job may be made larger in two dimensions—vertical and horizontal. Horizontal job enlargement means giving the job incumbent more of similar things to do. In 'widening' the task in this way, the decisions an individual must make remain at the same level, but there will be more of them.

The horizontal enlargement of work may be done with the intention of reducing the monotony of work, and thereby lessening recruitment, absenteeism, and turnover problems. However, such enlargement may become technically essential as changes in plant and equipment require the grouping of previously separated activities into one job.

Vertical job enlargement means giving the work role the responsibility for higher level activities and decisions which were previously undertaken by the rank above. This form of enlargement is most frequently done with the intention of permitting the employee access to higher level satisfaction (ego-satisfactions) which can be derived from greater responsibility (higher level decision-making) and achievement and recognition.

Job enrichment is vertical job enlargement, but is a practical technique derived from the motivation theories of Herzberg[1]. Herzberg's work (see chapter 4) rests on the two-factor theory of motivation. The contents of one factor are predominantly dissatisfiers (such as working conditions, policy, and administration), and their elimination does not result in substantial and long-term work satisfaction. The other factor is consistently related to work satisfaction and includes: responsibility, achievement, the work itself. It is these issues which are related to the content of what is done. Job enrichment seeks to change job content so that the individual can improve his performance and thereby gain the above satisfactions.

This is a term which covers both horizontal and vertical job enlargement, and is also used to refer to other changes in the content (e.g., a decrease) of a work role. It is also used to refer to work designs which focus on the group, whereas job enlargement and job enrichment tend to focus more on the individual.

All of these approaches to job redesign require an examination of the work (and its organizational context) through the eyes of managers, production engineers and behavioural scientists. Job design is essentially a multi-disciplinary problem and activity—the behavioural scientist is the newest and an increasingly frequent recruit to the design team.

Job enlargement, enrichment, and restructuring are practical approaches to improving work performance by focusing on the needs of the employee rather than exclusively the needs of the technology.

> By job design we mean specification of the contents, the methods and the relationships of jobs to satisfy the requirements of the technology and the organization as well as the social and personal requirements of the job holder. (L. E. Davis[2]).

It is this approach which requires management to change their perceptions of the man/work relationship against an organizational background which frequently will specify that:

(a) skill requirements are minimized,
(b) training time is minimized,
(c) immediate costs are minimized,
(d) existing union agreements are not 'upset',
(e) existing equipment and facilities layout are not disturbed.

Attempts to redesign work will usually require management to set aside such criteria, and so will demand changed attitudes and high levels of management involvement, as well as a preparedness to see short-term costs at a higher level.

Indeed it would be quite mistaken to assume that all attempts at job redesign are successful. Unless intended changes are examined in an organizational context, particularly in the light of the effect of the proposed changes on communications, statuses, pattern of interaction and social relationships, as well as in terms of the economic functioning of the enterprise, experiments may have serious unintended consequences. Alderfer[3] reports that in a job enlargement project, severe interpersonal problems were reported. On an incentive-based assembly line operation women employees were allowed to control the speed of the line.

As a result, their overall job satisfaction went up as did their pay. But repercussions throughout the plant also followed. Irritation grew between superintendent and foremen, engineers and foremen, and superintendent and engineers. Eventually the experiment was halted. The foremen and six of the eight girls participating in the enlargement left the organization.

The same author reported that while holders of enlarged jobs had high satisfaction with pay, a significantly higher satisfaction with the use of their skills and abilities, they reported significantly *lower* satisfaction with respect they received from superiors. The restructuring of their roles had effected the interpersonal relationships which had developed out of the previous role relationships.

In a literature search, Lawler[4] examined ten studies where jobs had been enlarged on both the horizontal and vertical dimensions, to see whether the effects of increased motivation, resulting from job content changes, was more likely to result in higher quality work than in higher productivity. He states:

> . . . every study showed that job enlargement did have some positive effect since every study reports that job enlargement resulted in higher quality work. However, only four out of ten studies report that job enlargement led to higher productivity. This provides support for the view that the motivational effects produced by job enlargement are more

likely to result in higher quality work than in higher productivity.

The number of factors which effect the man/job relationship are only now beginning to be understood. Far more experimental work is required to establish the nature of their interdependence in influencing work behaviour and job performance.

The practice of job enrichment has recently attracted much attention. Early work was carried out in the United States, but recently a major British chemical company has itself carried out a number of experiments[5].

The main aims of the experimental studies were to examine:

(a) the *Generality of the findings* of earlier applications of Herzberg's research findings;
(b) the *feasibility of making changes* in a variety of operational situations with a variety of individual abilities;
(c) the *consequences to be expected*—particularly in relation to the size of the gains, the consequences for the supervisor's job, and the management role.

The studies were conducted with groups of sales representatives, design engineers, experimental officers, production men, production foremen, and engineering foremen. Control groups were set up, and the changes introduced into the experimental groups gradually and as naturally as possible, without the subjects knowing that the changes were the object of an experimental study. The trial period, during which performance and satisfaction of the experimental and control groups were monitored, normally lasted a year and were never less than six months.

While naturally there were procedural differences with each experimental group, the intention to test out job enrichment was common to them all. More specifically, the intention was to improve task efficiency and human satisfaction with work by restructuring the job so that there was increased opportunity for personal achievement and recognition, more responsible and challenging work, and greater opportunity for individual advancement and growth. The conclusions drawn from the experiment indicate the generality of the theory upon which job enrichment is based, and that the theory is not specific to American culture. Changes can be made in a variety of operational situations—the experimenters did not encounter a situation where the operational risk was so high as to prevent passing responsibility down the line. It was not found necessary to make changes selectively to take account of variation in individual abilities and attitudes and, furthermore, the changes implemented amongst staff (and payroll) did not result in claims for higher pay and improved working conditions. The main consequence of the experiment was the demonstration that compared with the previous situation, *good or better work* was being done by people at a lower level in the organization and, while recognition is given to the difficulty of measuring gains financially, these were estimated to be substantial.

Earlier experimental work in job enrichment took place (among other companies) in the American Telephone and Telegraph Company (AT&T). A now classic study was concerned with a group of 104 young women working in the company's Treasury Department, who answered customer complaint letters concerning stocks and bonds. The problems raised and details sought by clients were often complex, and the company had therefore to employ intelligent, literate girls. Recognizing the inadequacy of previous efforts to reduce the turnover rate amongst these women, an experiment in job enrichment was set up. Five objectives for the change programme were established:

(1) Improve the quality of service:
(2) maintain and/or improve productivity levels;
(3) improve the labour turnover situation;
(4) lower costs;
(5) improve employee job satisfaction.

Job changes were introduced into the experimental groups (some control groups were established) at approximately the rate of one motivator a week.

These changes were:

(1) Subject matter experts were appointed for other members to consult;
(2) supervision was reduced and the location of supervision changed to the correspondents' desk;
(3) correspondents signed their own letters—previously all letters had been signed by the supervisor;
(4) verification of the letters, previously 100 per cent, was reduced to 10 per cent;
(5) the correspondents were permitted to answer clients' letters in a more informal and personalized manner.

These and other changes, introduced into the experimental group resulted, after a short period of low performance, in substantially higher index of customer service than that obtained by the control groups. Turnover was substantially reduced during the study period, and a larger proportion of promotions were being made out of the experimental groups than out of the controls. Furthermore, members of the experimental groups derived greater satisfaction from the job than the control groups.

Robert Ford[6] who reports on the job enrichment studies carried out at AT&T, notes that the estimated saving in the Treasury Department accomplished by late 1967, after eighteen months of development, amounted to over half a million dollars.

While academics find reasons for criticizing Herzberg's two-factor theory (methodological grounds mainly), and job enrichment is often ignored by the non-practitioner, its practical application has been well documented in a number of important instances, both in the United States and in Britain. There is the danger that it may become yet another management panacea. While Herzberg's theory appears new and indeed has novel aspects, there is nothing in job enrichment which is inconsistent with the schemes of job analysis and the concepts of job design, notably socio-technical analysis, which originated in Britain.

The one point about job enrichment which should be kept in mind is that it tends to operate with the focus on a single job, or a group of jobs, and is less concerned with 'pay and conditions', organization structure, communication and training, etc., that is, the wider aspects of organizational life which have to be taken into account in any programme of organization change. One of the limitations of using job enrichment is that most reported studies are isolated, that is, pin-pricks on the surface of organizational life, albeit interesting and significant ones. The growing interest in and popularity of job enrichment concepts is perhaps due to the fact that, because of its narrow focus on isolated tasks, it can be practised within the context of the existing organization structure. Wider organization change programmes, of which job enrichment simply forms a technique, may imply changes less acceptable to managers and indeed changes which are somewhat more radical and less easily measured than those at which job enrichment aims.

While job enrichment, with its missionary flavour, has attracted much attention, other work of a similar kind, and often involving changes of greater organizational complexity, perhaps involving union-management relationships or having consequences for the organizational structure, has been accomplished. It is beyond the scope of this book to describe all these experiments in detail, but the reader may find it interesting to know where to look for further guidance.

One of the most complex and significant job design experiments has already been referred to in chapter 4: the experiment with coal mining methods[7]. A. K. Rice[8] reported on job and organizational re-design in an Indian textile mill. A case study in productivity bargaining and job enlargement is reported by Stephen Cotgrove in *The Nylon Spinners*[9]. The two books which contain a number of interesting case studies on job enrichment are *New Perspectives in Job Enrichment*[10] and *Not by Bread Alone*[11]. Paul Hill in *Towards a New Philosophy of Management*[12] reports on the company development programme in Shell UK, and on job and organizational design experiments.

Many job design experiments are carried out which are never publicly reported. Most of these are attempts to redesign jobs, undertaken with less experimental caution and scientific objectives, and with more managerial involvement and commitment, and the participation of those affected by the changes. We have emphasized elsewhere the danger of prescriptions which are not based upon a thorough diagnosis, and so perhaps a diagnostic framework for examining jobs, with a statement of some principles to be observed in job design should conclude this discussion.

SOME PRINCIPLES FOR JOB DESIGN

Job design is concerned with putting tasks together in such a way that they satisfy a number of criteria: technical, economic, organizational, and social. In a number of empirical studies carried out in Scandinavia by the Tavistock Institute and the Institute for Work Research, Oslo, into the structure and process of industrial democracy, some hypotheses were developed relating to the psychological needs of people at work. These (reported in chapter 4) are too general to provide close guidelines for job design, but they have been elaborated into the following more detailed considerations.

Principles for the redesigning of jobs
At the level of the individual:

(a) *Optimum variety of tasks* within the job. Too much variety can be inefficient for training and production as well as frustrating for the worker. However, too little can be conducive to boredom or fatigue. The optimum level would be that which allows the operator to take a rest from a high level of attention or effort or demanding activity while working at another and, conversely, allow him to stretch himself and his capacities after a period of routine activity.

(b) *A meaningful pattern of task that gives to each job a semblance of a single overall task.* The tasks should be such that although involving different levels of attention, degrees of effort or kinds of skill, they are inter-dependent—that is, carrying out one task makes it easier to get on with the next or gives a better end result to the overall task. Given such a pattern, the worker can help to find a method of working suitable to his requirements and can more easily relate his job to that of others.

(c) *Optimum length of work cycle.* Too short a cycle means too much finishing and starting; too long a cycle makes it difficult to build up a rhythm of work.

(d) *Some scope for setting standards of quantity and quality of production and a suitable feedback of knowledge of results.* Minimum standards generally have to be set by management to determine whether a worker is sufficiently trained, skilled or careful to hold the job. Workers are more likely to accept responsibility for higher standards if they have some freedom in setting them and are more likely to learn from the job if there is feedback. They can neither effectively set standards nor learn if there is not a quick enough feedback of knowledge of results.

(e) *The inclusion in the job of some of the auxiliary and preparatory tasks.* The worker cannot and will not accept responsibility for matters outside his control. Insofar as the preceding criteria are met, then the inclusion of such 'boundary tasks' will extend the scope of the workers' responsibility and make for involvement in the job.

(f) *The tasks included in the job should include some degree of care, skill, knowledge or effort that is worthy of respect in the community.*

(g) *The job should make some perceivable contribution to the utility of the product for the consumer.*

At group level:

(h) *Providing for 'interlocking' tasks, job rotation or physical proximity where there is a necessary interdependence of jobs* (for technical or psychological reasons). At a minimum this helps to sustain communication and to create mutual understanding between workers whose tasks are interdependent and thus lessens friction, recriminations and 'scapegoating'. At best, this procedure will help to create work groups that enforce standards of co-operation and mutual help.

(i) *Providing for interlocking tasks, job rotation or physical proximity where the individual jobs entail a relatively high degree of stress.* Stress can arise from apparently simple things such as physical activity, concentration, noise or isolation if these persist for long periods. Left to their own devices, people will become habituated but the

113

effects of the stress will tend to be reflected in more mistakes, accidents and the like. Communication with others in a similar plight tends to lessen the strain.

(j) *Providing for interlocking tasks, job rotation or physical proximity where the individual jobs do not make an obvious perceivable contribution to the utility of the end product.*

(k) *Where a number of jobs are linked together by interlocking tasks or job rotation they should as a group:*

(i) Have some semblance of an overall task which makes a contribution to the utility of the product.

(ii) Have some scope for setting standards and receiving knowledge of results.

(iii) Have some control over the 'boundary tasks'.

Over extended social and temporal units:

(l) *Providing for channels of communication so that the minimum requirements of the workers can be fed into the design of new jobs at an early stage.*

(m) *Providing channels of promotion to foremen rank which are sanctioned by the workers.*

It is clearly implied in this list of principles that the redesigning of jobs may lead beyond the individual jobs to the organization of groups of workers and to the organization of support services (such as maintenance). The implications reach further than this, of course, and effect the design of the organization as a whole.

Job design, which has been the preserve of industrial engineers, will increasingly come to include social and psychological criteria as well as the conventional criteria of technical systems. Research studies already indicate the difficulty that may be encountered in attempting job redesign—difficulties that derive not solely from management attitudes but also from the job-holders, clerks, factory workers, etc., whose own perception of work, its rewards and organization may reflect their own habituation to the typical approaches of methods engineers, and to the assumption that work cannot be very different from what it is now. Indeed, faced with only low level satisfactions from work, or with the absence of the higher level satisfactions, there is some evidence to suggest that employees become 'maintenance' conscious, that is, concerned mainly to preserve the existing working arrangements. Thus changes in job design and experiments to enhance people's satisfaction and performance at work may meet with both resistance and scepticism. Especially this will be so where long experience of more conventional working arrangements has had predictable effects on attitudes to and perceptions of work.

In these circumstances job design and changes in job design will require highly participative/consultative approaches between employees and management in order that communications (including employee ideas, etc.) about, and commitment to, new job design can be fully developed.

REFERENCES

(1) Herzberg, F., Mausner, B., and Snyderman, B., *The Motivation to Work*, New York: Wiley, 1959.
and Herzberg, F., *Work and the Nature of Man*, Cleveland and New York: World Pub. Co., 1966.
(2) Davis, L. E., 'The Design of Jobs', *Tavistock Insititute of Human Relations Document*, No. T. 736, 1965.
(3) Alderfer, C. P., 'Job Enlargement and the Organizational Context', *Personnel Psychology*, **22**, 1969, 416-418.
(4) Lawler, E. E., 'Job Design and Employee Motivation', *Personnel Psychology*, **22**, 1969, 426-434.
(5) Paul, W., and Robertson, K., *Job Enrichment and Employee Motivation*, Gower Press, 1970.
(6) Ford, R. N., *Motivation Through the Work Itself*, New York: American Management Association, 1969.
(7) Trist, E. L., Higgin, G. W., Murray, H., and Pollock, A. B., *Organizational Choice: Capabilities of Groups at the Coal Face Under Changing Technologies*, Tavistock Publications, 1963.
(8) Rice, A. K., *Productivity and Social Organization: the Ahmedabad experiment*, Tavistock Publications, 1958.
(9) Cotgrove, S., Dunham, J., and Vamplew, C., *The Nylon Spinners*, George Allen & Unwin Ltd., 1971.
(10) Maher, J. R., (Ed.), *New Perspectives in Job Enrichment*, Van Nostrand Reinhold Company, 1971.
(11) King-Taylor, L., *Not by Bread Alone*, Business Books Ltd., 1972.
(12) Hill, P., *Towards a New Philosophy of Management*, Gower Press, 1972.
(13) Emery, F. E., and Thorsrud, E. *Form and Content in Industrial Democracy*, Tavistock Publications, 1969.

11
Organizational development

Trying to change an organization, or elements of it, in order to improve its functioning is as old as organization itself, and a major part of managements' task. Anyone who has been involved in work study, organization and methods, and training, knows that these activities were arrived at by attempts to improve productivity through new methods, arrangements, and skills. In a sense all were aimed at 'developing' the organization.

'Organizational Development' (O.D.) is different in that it is a planned and integrated approach to change which considers the organization as a whole. Traditional methods of changing and improving activities in organizations often take place in isolation and sometimes have a self-cancelling effect. Managers will be familiar with the confusion that results from different approaches to improved productivity; often these approaches are in competition with each other in the same organization. While method study is de-skilling jobs, the personnel department is introducing new procedures to combat absenteeism, and is also trying to eliminate, or reduce, some of the causes of labour turnover.

The familiar approaches to changing elements are still important, but it has been realized that, unless they are integrated, the organization will end up with at best only piece-meal improvements. It has been the development of the 'systems' approach to viewing organizations (see chapter 6) which has helped both behavioural scientists and management to see the necessity of approaching organizational change and development in an integrated and planned manner, with the total organization and the relationship to the environment as the primary perspectives.

Forces in the environment and the pressures which these forces place upon the organization have caused management to seek new approaches to improving individual performance. This leads to changes in management (e.g., knowledge, skills, and attitudes) and to changes in the organization's style of authority and procedures, which has in turn resulted in an extension of the process of management development into organizational development. Management development, as with all training in the past, has had its main focus on fitting the individual to the needs and practices of the organization. It is only relatively recently, with new evidence about the needs of people, that a concern has developed over adapting the organization to bring it more in line with the needs of the human resources within it.

The behavioural sciences have provided new insights, hypotheses and theories about man and work, and about change and the future. At the same time they have developed research methods, and have gained a degree of acceptance which make it possible for the behavioural scientist to work in organizations as change-agents as well as research scientists. When the behavioural scientist is acting as a change-agent he can be said to be involved in organizational development work as opposed to pure research. In the change-agent role the scientist is an 'active' person, acting, or assisting management to act, to introduce change. For this reason this 'active' form of on-going research which may have to be undertaken in less than scientifically favourable circumstances, is called 'action-research'. This activity leads to both substantive change in the *structure* of the enterprise, as well as to related learning on the part of management (and others) which change *process* aspects, e.g., interpersonal, and inter-group behaviour.

It has often been remarked that the researcher, in his quest for objective reality, for truth, and disengagement with that object which he is studying, is just as interested in the 'dead-body' as he is in the 'live-object'. O.D. specialists and action-researchers retain their need to remain objective (a good reason for them being outside consultants), but do not remain impartial to the organization's health. They acquire a commitment to the health of the organization and to its growth and survival. In that respect O.D. specialists not only become in a significant way *more* than an observer, but also introduce into the organization their own values, which as behavioural scientists will reflect their special concern with the organization as a 'social system', and the extent to which it meets the needs of people at their work.

Early organizational development theories, and indeed some current approaches, exhibit a well-defined value standpoint. To a degree this seems to depend on the generality or specificity with which they define the organization's environment. Perspectives which have taken into account general human needs and the (impending) overall social changes, have on the whole had stronger value standpoints (humanistic-democratic) than those which examine the organization's environment more specifically with detailed concern for actual markets, forms of technology, and the realities of existing differences in operation, and needs among sub-units and employees. In examining these aspects, O.D. has taken a systems orientation and moved nearer to a multi-disciplinary approach to change and development, particularly in the use of operational research (O.R.) methods. O.R. methods are often necessary to cope with the complexity of variables which systems models tend to generate, but there remains a distinction between O.D. and O.R., which Beckhard[1] noted:

> O.R. practitioners tend to select economic or engineering variables, certainly variables which are quantitative and measurable, and which appear to be linked directly to the profit and efficiency of the system ... The O.D. practitioner tends to be more concerned with the human variable and values.

Organizational development will in the future be an increasingly multi-disciplinary exercise. The early initiative in O.D. may have come from the behavioural sciences, but the concomitant analysis of markets, work methods, technology, will require other disciplines to act co-operatively with behavioural science, (and vice

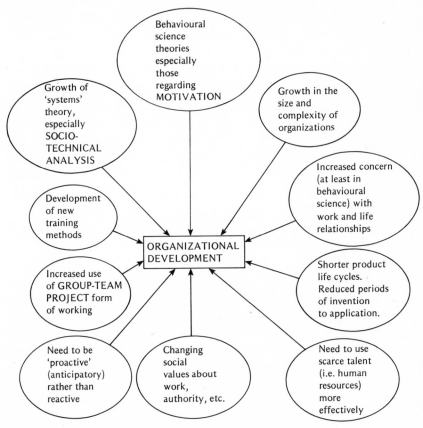

Fig. 11.1 *The pressures for organizations to change*

versa). However, the problems faced by many organizations at present appear to have brought into primary focus the necessity of examining the organization from the standpoint of the human resource. O.D. has been made possible by new methods both in research and training, and by new models which help in the understanding of the overall complexity of organizations. It has been made necessary by the nature of change itself, by rapidly changing environmental factors, by advances in technology, by shortened product life cycles, and, most important from the behavioural scientist's viewpoint, by the changes in people themselves.

Some of the perceived reasons for O.D. are indicated in Fig. 11.1. These reflect pressures from within and on the organization.

Early approaches to organizational development have their origins in the human relations school of the social sciences. The main point of attention and action has been up the interpersonal and inter-group relationships elements in work behaviour. The main concern of this approach has been to change an organization's culture—its system of beliefs and values—in order that the traditional mechanistic view of man at work, and authoritarian and directive management, can be replaced by new perceptions of man, and a more democratic management culture. This is sometimes referred to as the 'democratic-humanistic' ethos, and by sociologists as the 'normative-approach'. It tends to ignore factors in the organization's environment and the technology which may place a constraint on the choices open to the organization to develop new structures and processes in line with the human relations school 'panaceas'. It also tends to ignore significant differences in needs and expectations that can exist between groups of people. Some behavioural scientists have acknowledged openly that their participation in organizational development is an 'active' one which involves a social philosophy, and an attempt to produce, in the end, a more democratic and humane society.

THE HUMAN
RELATIONS
APPROACH

> Industrial social psychologists ... admit that in preaching 'human relations' they have been selling not so much a valid psychological theory, more a way of life, but have defended their approach on the grounds that it is a socially legitimized philosophy. Pugh[2].

and

> ... change-agents share a social philosophy, a set of values about the world in general and human organizations in

particular. More often than not, change-agents believe that the realization of these values will ultimately lead not only to a more humane and democratic system but to a more efficient one. Bennis[3].

Approaches to organizational development derived from the human relations movement are frequently prescriptive. Traditional forms of organization—the hierarchical and functionally specialized organizations (bureaucracies) are seen as unable to respond adequately to new conditions and unable to provide adequate opportunities for its members to grow, or to perform at a level equated with their potential. In Argyris' view[4] the typical contemporary form of organization fails to provide authentic relationships for the individual, as the relationships often lack openness and trust. His main theme is the need to integrate the individual into the organization in such a manner that mature, adult-like relationships between people, and between them and the organization, exist. These relationships should have the characteristics of openess, caring, trust, and participation. In this respect traditional organizations are characterized by low interpersonal competence. Argyris' main tool in his approach to improving the effectiveness of the organization is that of sensitivity training.

In some respects the development, and continued presence of the prescriptive-normative approach to organizational development is a counter-weight to the structural-mechanistic approaches advocated by the scientific management school, and still evidenced by the development of management sciences which concentrate on technical and control aspects of work situations, while studiously ignoring the human consequences of their organization and work designs.

HUMAN RESOURCES APPROACH— SOCIO-TECHNICAL DIAGNOSIS

In Europe contemporary concern with organizational development has been less prescriptive, and has implicitly echoed the criticism Leavitt[5] directed against the normative approach which universally emphasizes the dilution of power in organizations, and advocates a shift from 'coercion-compromise' management to 'collaboration-consensus' management:

Besides the belief that one changes people first, these power equalization approaches ... for example centrally concerned with affect; with morale, sensitivity, psychological security ... they place much value on human growth and fulfilment as well as upon task accomplishment; and they have often stretched the degree of causal connection between the two.

Some of the most influential research work concerning organizational theory has been done in Britain, foremost in this being the work carried out at the Tavistock Institute of Human Relations. Their now classic study of the longwall method of coalmining[6], in which they were able to examine the effect of a mass-production coalface technology upon the multi-skilled 'craft' miner, and in which they proposed alternative forms of work organization, resulted in the development of a major concept in organizations theory—the socio-technical system. This has been explained elsewhere (chapters 5 and 6), but its significance lies in that it integrated the perspective of the social-theorist (the human relations school) and that of the scientific management theorist (the methods engineer). Today, this has led to the development of a sub-discipline of the behavioural sciences—Organizational Behaviour:

> An emerging interdisciplinary quasi-independent science, drawing primarily on the disciplines of psychology and sociology, but also on economics, operational research and production engineering. Pugh[2].

The interdependence of the social system of an organization (which is the prime, and often, only focus of the human relations school) with the technical system, pointed to the variability of organization and job designs that are possible and indeed necessary from the standpoint of both the needs of people and the needs of the task. Later work emerging from the Tavistock (Emery[7], Miller and Rice[8]) elaborated the systems concept of organization. These elaborations included models of environmental situations which organizations may face, and which, with internal variables, such as size and technology, contribute to a potentially wide range of organizational forms which may be imperative to ensure the primary task of survival.

The work of Joan Woodward[9] has also demonstrated the wide range of organizational forms which are in large part a consequence of differing environmental constraints and production technologies. In her study of manufacturing companies in south-east Essex Joan Woodward was able to show that the number of people reporting to the chief executive, the number of management levels in the hierarchy, and the number of people supervised by first line management varies significantly with differing forms of manufacturing technology. Companies which could be regarded as 'successful' tended to cluster around the median measure for these structural variables, suggesting that successful companies in differing technologies were constrained by elements in the task to assume certain organizational forms.

Other work, notably that of Burns and Stalker[10], has supported that of Tavistock and Woodward, to demonstrate emphatically that there must be concern with the organization as a whole—it is a system of work activities (including the technology), and a social system. There must be concern with the organization in its relationship with the environment—it cannot be treated as an isolated entity. Organizations are dynamic things and their stability and change involve the understanding of complex relationships between the technical system, the social system and the firm's environment.

THE SADLER-
BARRY STUDY
IN THE
PRINTING
INDUSTRY

It is this viewpoint which Sadler and Barry adopted in their study[11], and it exemplifies the empirical approach to organizational development. The researchers chose the printing industry after studies showed it to be in need of rapid adjustment to changing conditions. In this context, the prime objectives of the research were:

- to attempt to relate current theory of management and organization to the problems facing family businesses;
- to find an opportunity to test out ideas stemming from social science research in industry and especially to test the techniques of action research.

Their book describes the programme of action-research in a printing group from the autumn of 1964 to late 1967. As industrial sociologists concerned with the study of human behaviour at work in a situation of change, the researchers set out to observe and describe a firm from four points of view:

(1) its technology;
(2) the beliefs, values, traditions and patterns of social relationships which together make up the social system of the firm;
(3) the formal structure of the organization;
(4) the relation between the enterprise and its environment.

These are the four major interrelated causal dimensions of organizational life.

In terms of the business performance of the printing group, the organization was seen to be in a

strong position relative to the average firm in industry. Its sales and profits were expanding and it enjoyed relatively high productivity. The only unsatisfactory aspect of its performance was its relatively high level of manpower costs.

Early research showed wide differences in the way in which the organization should have functioned in theory and how it actually did in practice. Formal organizational relationships were the subject of considerable error on the part of many managers, and informal arrangements infrequently contradicted the formal structure (see Figs. 5.2 and 5.3 in chapter 5). Such was the importance of this informal structure that the working of the system appeared to rely heavily on personalities and feelings of teamwork among managers.

> This was exemplified by the extremely uneven pattern of communications in the firm. There appeared to be a strong case for recognizing the force and value of these informal arrangements and for modifying the formal organization structure to take account of them.

Additionally there were problems in the relationship between sales and production, and between the day and night shifts. Furthermore, the company lacked functions which were important to the growth and development of the business, notably, management accounting, market research, and training. These vital activities manage the 'boundaries' of the enterprise and keep it tuned into important aspects of its performance vis-à-vis the environment.

The process of action-research took the social scientist beyond mere recommendations.

> There was no question of presenting a fixed set of recommendations to management on a take-it-or-leave-it basis. The procedure which developed was much more a process of influence with the influence flowing in both directions.

The programme of organizational change eventually agreed with management fell into two categories—short term adjustment and long term development. In developing the programme of change the social scientists' specific contribution was to examine the organization structure in terms of the contributions of the informal and formal systems for getting the tasks done. Specifically, the researchers took six steps:

- examined the work flow to see what relationships were needed,
- decided where the formal organization met the requirements and where it did not,
- found out what informal methods of coping existed,
- found out what formal channels existed to facilitate relationships outside of the chain of command and evaluated their effectiveness,

- decided which informal methods to formalize,
- devised ways of facilitating those which were best left to operate informally.

The short term adjustments involved, among other things, adapting the organization structure to fit more closely the actual flow of communications on work matters. Steps were also taken to reduce the emphasis on hierarchical control and to spread communications more evenly across the organization. Problems of inter-shift relationships were also examined and steps taken to integrate them. Status levels were made clearer, since it had been found that ambiguity on status issues aroused anxiety and were a source of confusion in organizational relationships. Further appointments were made to relieve the directors of day to day concern with the internal workings of the organization.

The evaluation that the researchers carried out as an interim measure showed that the changes implemented had met the objectives stated but had inevitably aroused feelings, particularly among those whose informal status position or proximity to top management had been affected.

In this programme of organizational development the researchers provided expertise in organizational analysis which helped management to analyse the problems and institute, along with the researchers, the necessary changes. At the same time, the researchers themselves learned not only the relevance of aspects of organizational theory, but about the reality of business problems as well. This does not imply the elimination of formal management training schemes, but it does demonstrate that changes in organizational life must come not only as a result of changing people's attitude and behaviour through training, but also from structural changes, that is, changes in the roles that people have to play, such that better and changed performance is both encouraged and reinforced. Such a programme of changes requires the integration of training activities with the design of organizations as systems.

CONCLUSIONS   The organizational development work of Bennis and Argyris has used more universal approaches to organizational change and has been less concerned with diagnosis. They have tended to focus mostly on educational intervention. Lawrence and Lorsch[12] state that they

> seem to recognize intellectually these systemic properties of organization ... in practice, they put less emphasis on addressing them explicitly.

Recognition of the systemic properties of organization requires greater attention to the process of *diagnosing* an organization's situation and the complex of forces which make it what it is. It should be a thorough diagnosis, which time or other operational pressures frequently cause management to neglect, and yet without it the subsequent phases of any O.D. programme are at great risk. The sequence below indicates the importance of diagnosis, as what follows is dependent upon it.

DIAGNOSIS——→PRESCRIPTION——→ACTION——→EVALUATION

What should be prescribed can only be adequately derived from a thorough-going diagnosis. What strategies and tactics may be involved in the *action* phase can only be judged from an adequate knowledge of the organization's situation. *Evaluation* (effect of action) can only take place if the starting point is known.

A 'presenting symptom' can be the starting point for co-operation between management and behavioural scientists in work of organizational change, and it is in the search for, and examination of, the probably numerous inter-dependent causes of the symptom (e.g., problem relationships between departments, perceived low performance, morale, growth, high turnover of employees, reducing market share), that the behavioural scientist will utilize:

(a) research methods—to generate data

   and

(b) concepts, models and theories of organizational behaviour to guide his data collection and interpretation.

In the circumstances of locating the cause of a particular organizational problem, the O.D. practitioner will reduce the scope of his analytical and diagnostic activities. It is likely, however, that increasingly organizations will initiate organizational studies and development programmes which are responses to the much wider problem of coping with the future, of anticipating social, economic and technological change with new organizational forms. In this latter case the diagnostic process is bound to be a more comprehensive process, which commences with the organization/environment relationship.

(1) Beckhard, R., *Organizational development strategies and models*, New York: Addison Wesley, 1969.   REFERENCES

125

(2) Pugh, D. S., 'Organizational Behaviour: an approach from psychology'. In G. Heald (ed.) *Approaches to the Study of Organizational Behaviour*, London: Tavistock Publications. 1970.

(3) Bennis, W. G., *Organizational Development: Its nature, origin and prospects*, New York: Addison Wesley, 1969.

(4) Argyris, C., *Integrating the Individual and the Organization*, New York: Wiley, 1964.

(5) Leavitt, H. J., 'Applied Organizational Change in Industry: Structural, Technological and Humanistic Approaches,' In J. March (ed.) *Handbook of Organizations*, Chicago: Rand McNally, 1965.

(6) Trist, E. L., Higgin, G. W., Murray, H., and Pollock, A. B., *Organizational Choice: Capabilities of Groups at the Coal Face Under Changing Technologies*, Tavistock Publications, 1963.

(7) Emery, F. E., (ed.), *Systems Thinking*, Harmondsworth: Penguin, 1969.

(8) Miller, E. J., and Rice, A. K., *Systems of Organization: Task and Sentient Systems and their Boundary Control*, London: Tavistock Publications, 1967.

(9) Woodward, J., *Industrial Organizations: Theory and Practice*, Oxford University Press, 1965.

(10) Burns, T., and Stalker, G. M., *The Management of Innovation*, Tavistock Publications, 1961.

(11) Sadler, P. J., and Barry, B. A., *Organizational Development: Case Studies in the Printing Industry*, Longmans, 1970.

(12) Lawrence, P. R., and Lorsch, J. W., *Developing Organizations: Diagnosis and Action*, New York: Addison Wesley, 1969.

An afterword

This book has attempted to outline some aspects of behavioural science, looking at some theories and at some applications in the industrial organization. Compared with the physical and medical sciences, the amount of investment in behavioural and social science research is very small, but even so, the amount of information so far generated is such that considerable specialization has already taken place. Social and behavioural scientists themselves can scarcely keep up with the new developments, so it is especially difficult for a manager to do so, who is already faced with many other specialists' claims to his attention in order to make his role more effective. There is always the danger that, faced with complexity and too much information, the manager will draw away from specialist advice and rely on hunch alone.

It is hoped that the content of this book has helped to provide the reader with a diagnostic framework with which to handle complexity. In the future, organizations will increasingly find themselves using behavioural scientists to seek information about the organization, to diagnose problems, and help introduce changes. These activities will vary widely, but whatever the change objectives, from simple modification in work flow and paper communication to more radical changes in organization objectives and values, the manager will find himself having to work with the behavioural scientists, and with behavioural science concepts. The word 'with' must be emphasized. In the past most consultancy and advice has ended with someone doing something *to* somebody. If change programmes of a kind to engage more of the individual in the organization's activities and objectives are to be realistic, then they must commence with the orientation of doing things *with* people in a participative way. This is only possible if the manager comprehends and welcomes the additional understanding that the behavioural sciences can bring to his role.

The acceptance of the role of the behavioural scientist in the organization depends upon the manager having 'a feel' for behavioural sciences and understanding its approach. He must also, of course, be able to accept the values which under-pin behavioural sciences.

All sciences are, ultimately, expressions of values—beliefs in what is fundamentally right or wrong. Values under-pin the political system, the educational system, indeed under-pin society. The use to which any scientific information is put is also an expression of values, a reflection of what the users believe to be the appropriate (even morally right) goals for a social system. Accordingly, it would be inappropriate to conclude this book without discussing some of the important issues about the future application of the behavioural sciences.

The selectivity with which information was gathered to write the preceeding chapters is in itself a reflection of the biases and values of the authors. It is appropriate that these should be made more explicit. Many of the problems faced today both in organizations and in society are those of integrating people's activities. Considerable attention has historically been given to the means by which people's activities may be *controlled*, but less attention has been paid to the *way* in which the individual's activities might be integrated, both in relation to his colleagues and in relationship to the wider objectives of the social system to which he belongs.

Technology has provided impressive and perhaps dauntingly new facilities for people to communicate, see and share events with each other, to learn rapidly, to live longer, and travel faster. Technology has helped people to overcome many of the problems of scarcity. Lack of political integration and shared values, however, prevents nations dispensing with huge expenditures on defence systems which, if released for use elsewhere into society, would further the eradication of world-wide scarcity and contribute towards a growth in education, housing, medicine, and social planning, etc. However, technical advances have tended to determine the nature of educational development, with the effect that education tends to provide technology with the manpower it needs to further itself. Consequently there has not been a comparable advance in our competence and skill as a society to handle the rapidly increasing power which technology gives us. Technology has therefore contributed very significantly to the many social problems which as a society we do not know how to handle. Withdrawal from work is matched more seriously by withdrawal from society both physically and emotionally. In such circumstances the rejection of authority, which some regard as extremely serious, is a symptom of a deeper cause concerned with the nature of society itself.

The present social order is one which largely rests on things being done to people and for them. Technical advances to be most effective require the development of institutions which can meet the new needs which have been created by the new conditions. Such needs when not met by organizations and by political systems, which may be unaware of them and structured to preserve traditional notions of authority, often give rise to apathetic and aggressive behaviour. It then of course becomes increasingly difficult to introduce participation since the rejection of ideas and activities which may help to change situations take on an emotional strength. The technical and economic advances which have been made in organizations and in society have not been matched by advances in social systems for handling power, influence, opportunity, etc. The emphasis placed on the *individual* to be responsible, hard working, high achieving, etc. is strong, and is reflected in the efforts of education and training to stimulate the individual to better performances *as an individual.* Maslow's hierarchy of needs has as its two highest level needs *self* esteem and *self* actualization and these are reinforced by our culture as people are 'liberated', mainly through economic, educational, and technical advance.

The reality of a society, or indeed of an organization, is the integration of the individual's life and activities with that of others. This means not only influencing other people but being prepared *to be influenced* by others. People will generally only be influenced if they *share* values and common objectives, unless of course repressive methods are employed.

Consequently the growing concern of society and organization is integration—the development of effective inter-dependence among people who in the West are relatively free from scarcity. This cannot be effectively achieved coercively. Inter-dependence means sharing. In this light it is probably essential for organizations to devolve relevant power and authority and to spread influence and responsibility. At the level of society this of course implies a far greater spread of political power within the framework of a people who are highly educated and a technology which is very complex. Alienation from the political system because one feels powerless to influence it, or because it seems worthless to attempt to contribute to it, can have serious consequences for society, just as alienation from work can have serious consequences for the organization.

There are two crucial issues in which behavioural science must play a part. First a picture or model of society must be conveyed to people at large, particularly those who have power and influence, which incorporates the beliefs mentioned above. Too frequently today, in the authors' opinion, do we witness critical decisions being taken by well-intentioned people, which are based on premises about society and human behaviour which are seriously out of date.

Second, having succeeded in helping to convey to people a relevant model of society and human behaviour, a great deal of help will be needed to implement new policies and practices based on these new premises. This is the 'how' of behavioural science, and as experience is accumulated and recorded, the 'how' may well be vital if the inevitable change is to be dealt with in a civilized and stable way.

Index

132

134

Printed by William Clowes & Sons Limited, London, Colchester and Beccles